SHADE

Keith Wiley

SHADE

planting solutions for shady gardens

TIMBER PRESS

SHADE
Keith Wiley

Published in North America in 2006 by
Timber Press, Inc.
The Haseltine Building
133 S.W. Second Avenue, Suite 450
Portland, Oregon 97204-3527, U.S.A.
www.timberpress.com

A catalog record for this book is available from
the Library of Congress.

ISBN-13: 978-0-88192-755-9
ISBN-10: 0-88192-755-4

While all reasonable care has been taken during the preparation
of this edition, neither the publisher, editors, nor the authors
can accept responsibility for any consequences arising from
the use thereof or from the information contained therein.

Commissioning Editor: Michèle Byam
Art Editor: Victoria Burley
Design: Kate Ward
Editor: Joanna Chisholm
Picture Research: Emma O'Neill
Production: Gary Hayes

Set in Joanna MT

Printed and bound in China by
Toppan Printing Company Limited

Half title page: Toad lily (*Tricyrtis rochebrunianum*), a perennial
found in moist woodland.

Title page: This mixed planting in a shady American garden includes
ornamental grasses.

This page: *Acer, Hosta,* and *Galium odoratum* in shady woodland
in Beth Chatto's garden, Chelmsford, Essex.

CONTENTS

INTRODUCTION

A garden without shade is incomplete, somehow diminished of the magic that dappled light and dark shadows bring to even the most mundane of sites.

LEFT John Tordoff's garden in London is an amazing example of what an artistic plantsman can achieve in a confined space. The cluttered, homely style in the foreground is balanced by the simple green garden beyond the arch, where the high bamboo screen and wisteria brilliantly obscure surrounding houses.

Shady parts of a garden are often perceived as difficult or awkward places to deal with. Perhaps this wariness of shade is hardly surprising in climates as fickle as that of northern Europe, as I am sure shade is wholeheartedly embraced in gardens in sunnier parts of the world such as the Mediterranean or southern USA.

If you approach your plans for shady areas in a positive frame of mind, they can become precious and valuable parts of any garden. For those like myself who are trying to make a garden on a new site in an exposed open field, I yearn with a passion for shaded nooks where I can escape the occasional spells of blazing sunshine. Yet even here, with a little ingenuity, shade can be deliberately created and incorporated into the general garden design, so that some of the wonderful plants which prefer these conditions can be grown and in the process provide a cool retreat for the gardener as well.

Differing shade conditions

Shade in the context of this book covers everything from almost full sun with just a few hours of shading each day to spots where the sun rarely if ever penetrates. It also varies from moist sites to ones that are almost bone-dry.

You should be aware that the light levels in these shady locations are just one aspect of the growing conditions there, as far as any plants are concerned. For plants, the soil conditions, how many tree roots there are in the ground, and how much wind whistles past may be of more significance than how much direct light falls on them. These various elements act together to provide the whole shady environment, and no one condition is significantly more important than any other. In other words, you should try to evaluate the site as a whole as much as you can. If you do this, the design options are frequently narrowed down to the point where a solution becomes almost glaringly obvious.

LEFT Water and iris form a restful if slightly uninspired combination in the Nitobe memorial garden of the UBC Botanical Garden in British Colombia. The duckweed floating among the water lilies is a real problem in shady ponds in which water does not circulate freely.

Why cherish shade?

When a house or a building is included on a site containing a garden, it is very rare for there to be no shady areas. There will nearly always be a shaded side to the house, alongside a boundary fence, or under an established tree or trees. These are relatively large areas of shade. At the other end of the scale, a single large container standing on the ground creates a small amount of shade on one side.

You may out of necessity have to deal with your current shady conditions because that is all you have, yet experienced and accomplished gardeners sometimes go out of their way to create such shaded spots, even if initially they did not exist.

If you are not of ardent plantsman persuasion, you may well ask, "Why bother to cherish shade at all?" I believe the answer may be that shade introduces to any garden, very

simply and quickly, a mood and atmosphere that can border on the magical. Think of words that might be used to describe a shaded part of a garden. If you are having a bad day, you might come up with examples such as "dank", "draughty", "dull", "damp", and "dark". All of these negative connotations can and will be addressed in the following chapters. More likely, however, in more positive moments words such as "relaxing", "restful", "calming", and "sanctuary" are going to be coined, and I hope to show how these positive feelings can be encouraged and enhanced in your planting schemes.

There is another reason for cherishing shade which I have deliberately held back on for fear of tempting those of you who simply do not have the right set of shady conditions to go in this particular direction. When soil and light levels are conducive, these shaded areas can accommodate a vast range of plant species, some of which are among the most beautiful you can grow, if your tastes are attuned to them. Many plants native to the Orient come from wooded areas and they have, to my eyes, a simplicity and elegance that lifts my spirits just by looking at them. I personally love the simplicity of form of many shade-lovers such as the erythroniums and British natives such as bluebells, wood anemones, and snowdrops.

I value as well their lifestyles – common to many woodlanders – of appearing in spring and then having a long siesta when the tree canopy closes over. Somehow this truncated season means that I never grow tired of them as they are nearly always fresh when above ground. It is a bit like a beautiful celebrity tragically dying young at the peak of their beauty. He or she remains forever young and lovely in our memories and never has to suffer any indignities of growing old.

There is a practical benefit to this as well, in that while the plants are having a rest below ground so can you above it. Having areas of your garden where the plants are above ground for only three or four months a year introduces seasonal variety and heightens and enhances the child-like anticipation of the approaching spring. You are more likely to attune your internal body clock to the rhythms of the changing seasons if your garden emphasizes this seasonality.

The only down side to this is that this form of gardening can become compulsive, even addictive, and you can start to crave even more shaded areas to cultivate.

BELOW The country garden style is here confined to a narrow space, which is only lightly shaded. Many of the plants, including *Cortaderia richardii* in the left foreground, would struggle to flower as well without an extensive sight of the sky. Narrow grass paths also require a great deal of light if they are to remain in good condition.

BELOW *Erythronium* 'Jeanette Brickell' is a hybrid of the white form of *E. oregonum*, which grows in the woods of Washington state and British Colombia. The aristocratic erythroniums are often called fawn lilies, because many of them have mottled leaves.

RIGHT The very essence of an English woodland in spring is encapsulated by bluebells in full flower alongside a snaking path, with trees burgeoning into glorious emerald and the birds in full song, having recently returned from their winter migration.

Woodlanders in the open

I had this problem in my last garden, because I acquired ever more woodland plants and then did not have the shaded locations to grow them all. Out of desperation I planted many out in full sun, albeit on a north-facing slope, which the garden occupied. To my surprise, most grew really well and actually generally flowered better than in shadier conditions. English bluebells, such as those shown opposite, are a case in point. Usually considered a quintessentially north European woodland plant, the best I have ever seen in flower are found on the high open moorland of Dartmoor, with hardly a tree in sight.

The fact that the climate is damp in this corner of south-west England probably partly explains why I can get away with planting woodlanders in more open positions, yet the north-facing slope is also important. Having moved just down the road to a new south-facing slope, the same plants that thrived before in full sun have showed signs of stress in the more direct and stronger sunlight of the south slope.

The moral of this story is probably just to experiment with growing plants in different places, as well as treating the written words of gardening authors as guidelines only, for our gardening conditions are infinitely varied. Plants often have a gloriously rebellious streak to fly in the face of accepted truths, but woodlanders in sun are rarely as luxurious and happy as those growing in shadier conditions.

There is a world of difference between a plant surviving in the open and one thriving in conditions more akin to its native habitat. If you can create the right environment, then seeing your plants flourish in dappled light is a truly memorable experience.

SHADE IN GARDENS

WILD WOODLAND SHADE

There is no better way to start studying shade in its myriad aspects than by looking at the various types of natural woodland.

PREVIOUS PAGES With climbing plants, including *Rosa* 'Bobbie James', scrambling over every vantage point, an air of unruly wildness has here been engendered. Clues such as a lack of weeds, swept path, and carefully sited pots show that the garden has not, however, been abandoned.

LEFT The maples of New England are justifiably famed for their fabulous fall colour. Here in Maine innumerable young seedlings make it seem as if the forest floor is carpeted with a thick layer of fallen leaves. However, such fast-growing seedlings will rapidly become too dominant for spring flowers to flourish.

Plants that prefer shaded conditions are often referred to as woodlanders, yet everyone has a different mental image of what constitutes a woodland. In many cases, this image will be dictated by the natural woods which are in the vicinity of where they live, and this can be amazingly different from place to place.

In California and up the Pacific north-west of America and Canada grow widely spaced pine trees, oak chaparral, woods of garry oak or dense, dark conifer woods, redwoods, or otherwise. In the UK there are a similar range of woodland habitats from the mixed woods of places such as the New Forest to forestry plantations and natural stands of Scots pines in the Lake District and in Scotland. The conditions that occur in all of these are very different from each other, not just in the amount of light reaching the ground but also in the varying soils.

Studying and looking more closely at these different woodlands can help you to grow woodlanders more successfully. Opening your minds to nuances of natural woods will make you ever more aware of the beauty and spirituality of your sylvan inheritance. It can also help to maximize the benefits of shaded areas in your own garden.

Wild woods as gardens?

Try a mental exercise of looking at woodland and wondering whether you could create a good garden underneath its trees. After the initial surge of enthusiasm of how wonderful this imaginary garden may look, details such as there being too many rocks, not enough soil, too much shrubby undergrowth, and a range of other considerations start to kick in as the reality of attempting this make-over dawns. A good indicator of whether such a woodland garden might be feasible is by noticing what plants are already growing there. The presence of a lot of herbaceous plants suggests that the soil is good, the

LEFT This wood in Maryland with its oaks and tulip trees contains typical alluvial-soil plants. It produces little native understorey growth and its canopy trees are late leafing out, and thus provide perfect conditions for spring-flowering perennials and bulbs.

ABOVE In mid-spring, erythroniums and fritillaries revel in the deep rich leafy soil of this wood in northern Oregon. By early summer, the trees have fully leafed out, yet they still allow enough sunlight to filter through so plants can grow at ground level.

inevitable tree roots not too shallow and that there is sufficient light to grow at least spring flowering plants. In other words, the easiest and best gardening conditions prevail. Would the possibility of removing some of the lower tree branches let even more light in, allowing you to grow an even wider range of plants? A large number of shrub species under the tree canopy indicates that the woodland still has possibilities as a woodland garden but that it would be a lot more difficult to make.

Consider the woods pictured here. Those in Maryland (*top right*) support an incredible range of plants on the forest floor in spring and early summer. These spring ephemerals include trilliums, cardamines, dicentras, and smilacinas as well as a mass of other very familiar plants that I grow in my own garden. Such giant woodland "gardens" occur because

the canopy trees are tall and very late leafing out, and there are very few understorey trees or shrubs to prevent the sunlight from reaching the ground. From the plants' point of view at ground level, this must be as close to nirvana as it gets, with maximum light in the spring, shelter from the wind, a rich leaf-mould soil to grow in, and large protective leaves high overhead in the summer to keep them cool. No wonder so many plants thrive in such growing conditions.

A similar wood (*top left*) on the western side of the North American continent, in Oregon, demonstrates how light is still reaching the ground even when the canopy has leafed out. Once again, with few understorey trees and shrubs to cut out light and riddle the soil with their roots, a similarly shaded area in your garden would not present any major problems for growing a wide range of plants, even though the canopy is almost continuous.

Conifers are often a major cause of anxiety because of the dense shade under their canopy and their capacity for making the ground very dry beneath them. However, when they are as widely spaced as these (*below*) are in Scotland, they would be an asset to any garden. When spread out like this, shade from such conifers is limited to patches, with large areas between the trees receiving full sun for large parts of the day. In very broad terms, the more light striking the ground for at least part of the year, the wider the range of plants you can grow there.

RIGHT Pine trees, such as these Scots pine growing in Rothiemurchus forest in Scotland, are very common throughout the northern hemisphere. When mature, they provide perfect high shade for gardening below.

RIGHT The shading in this Scottish plantation during summer is quite dense, but because deciduous larch trees grow among the evergreen pines a significant amount of light is able to reach the ground five or six months of the year. This creates perfect light conditions for woodland gardening and enables grasses to grow.

COUNTRY GARDENS

If there is any one thing which differentiates a country garden from other types, it will be the greater amount of space available to the gardener.

LEFT Although Spanish bluebells (*Hyacinthoides hispanica*) will happily grow in full sun, they look in their element here beneath the shade of *Acer palmatum* 'Kasagiyama' at The Garden House in Devon. The tightly clipped cotoneaster hedge and the paved path provide a sense of order to an otherwise wild-looking planting scheme.

A major benefit of the extra space in a country garden is to allow those who make gardens in shaded areas of their land to capture some of the atmospheric tranquillity of native woods and to encourage a more naturalistic approach to planting.

Naturalistic planting, or planting which looks like it could occur somewhere in the natural world, is a relatively recent trend in garden planting styles. However, one of the few areas where it has been evident in established gardens in the past has been in woodland plantings. There, this style was and still is almost the norm, the traditional way of planting for shaded areas. Such a style may partly have come about because of the practicalities of gardening on this larger scale, with plants that succeed being encouraged and welcomed by the garden owners. The result is that woodland areas often have certain plants growing really well and smaller groups of many others – a characteristic of natural woods.

Larger groups

I am an ardent fan of massed planting of almost any plant, as it reminds me of how spectacular effects are created in nature by wildflowers, whether these are from humble daisies, celandines, or speedwell to more exotic species such as orchids or whistling Jacks (*Gladiolus communis* subsp. *byzantinus*). When you start to get a taste for wildflowers in other parts of the world, you raise the potential for exotic effect a good number of notches.

The extra space that country gardeners usually have at their disposal allows them to grow larger numbers of the same species together and to capture in some small way the beauty of how they may look in the wild. However, in our gardens (and whisper this silently) it is occasionally possible to grow some species better than in the wild, because they are watered and fed, and competing weeds are removed. For example, *Erythronium helenae* is known from only a few locations in

woodland garden near Chelmsford, Essex, the self-seeding in these views would suggest the plants were growing in a country garden. Such self-seeding trait is not one that you would recommend to an urban gardener with tight space constraints.

Likewise, allowing plants to create drifts and bands of colour, partly as a result of self-seeding but not exclusively so, is another luxury that the country gardener can employ. This drift planting technique can be deliberately used to engender a natural atmosphere to a garden and is especially useful in medium- to large-scale plantings in shady areas, being reminiscent of wild woods. The extravagant colours of the candelabra primulas draw the eye (right), but notice how the foliage of the fern and iris also drift through the scene, and how the hostas have been dot-planted but still leave the composition harmonious and restful. Candelabra primulas like damp conditions, and from a practical viewpoint these same damp, shady conditions will also make the wooden planks of the bridge extremely slippery, hence the fine-mesh wire-netting stretched on top.

The same drifting technique of naturalistic planting has also been introduced in the two

California, but where it does grow it can be seen in countless thousands. The vast majority of plants there bear only one flower per bulb (occasionally there may be two, and very rarely three), yet when growing well in cultivation this species will be twice the height of its wild counterparts and will carry up to six or seven flowers per stem.

Self-seeding

One of the features of a naturalistic style is the chance to let plants self-seed. Even had I not known they were taken in Beth Chatto's

BELOW The spurge *Euphorbia amygdaloides* var. *robbiae* casts a frothy yellow haze under hazel bushes in the "nuttery" at Sissinghurst, in early summer. The fresh green fronds of ferns add to the general light airiness of the planting.

gardens on these two pages. Many of the grand woodland gardens in the UK and elsewhere employ evergreen azaleas to create spectacular spring displays, such as those in the Savill gardens (*left*) in Windsor, and vast numbers of visitors are attracted to these kaleidoscopic shows. To many people, this spring extravaganza of rhododendrons flowering is what country woodland gardens are all about.

Even in small areas, evergreen azaleas are invaluable planted singly, in small groups, or in drifts. Their overall habit as they mature is often gently arching from central upright

trunks, and this is the same general shape of so many woodland perennials such as hellebores and cardamines. Their small leaves as well do not overpower even the smallest bulb, and this all results in evergreen azaleas complementing most plantings.

Sissinghurst "nuttery"

The effects created in the "nuttery" at Sissinghurst in Kent are altogether more subtle (*below*). Here, the local alkaline soils meant that growing massed ranks of evergreen azaleas was not an option, so the spring display here is

LEFT *Smilacina formosana* has recently been introduced by the Wynn-Jones' at Crug Farm Plants in Wales. This rare species is an elegant oriental member of the false Solomon's seals, which are common in North American woods.

RIGHT Welsh poppies (*Meconopsis cambrica*) thrive in quite dense shade at Hidcote in Gloucestershire. I love their orange and lemon colour mix, although this species will seed true to its individual colouring if its varieties are kept apart. There is also a less robust, orange-red variety, *M.c.* 'Frances Perry'.

interest and colour later in the season, plant it in small groups, leaving wide gaps between for taller, summer-flowering perennials or bulbs such as lilies and camassias.

Such gaps could also be planted up with early spring-flowering plants such as hellebores, primroses, and snowdrops. In this way you could produce a series of flowering events throughout the year and still remain true to the naturalness of the general design of the garden.

Maximizing use of space

I loved the Welsh poppies (*Meconopsis cambrica*) at Hidcote (right) not only for their cool colouring but also for the secrecy of their location. They are tucked in behind other shrubs bordering the path in part of the garden that could have been left unplanted. Yet by removing the lower branches of the overhead shrub and raising the canopy, the gardeners here have created a space for planting, which is a bonus.

This sort of spot would also be perfect for growing other early flowering plants from snowdrops and hellebores to erythroniums, trilliums, and epimediums. About the end of

PREVIOUS PAGES The style of this much-loved and cared-for plantsman's garden can readily be imitated because colour groupings and combinations are less important than the diversity of plants grown. Such a garden will give its owners countless hours of pleasure.

centred on perennials and bulbs. The sea of yellow and green produced by the spurge between the avenue of coppiced hazels looks very natural, with the placing of the statue a masterly addition. As the obvious point of reference for the eye, its scale makes the whole area of the garden seem much larger than it actually is.

This spurge is quite vigorous in its running habit, so to create this effect and still have some

LEFT Bowles' golden grass (*Milium effusum* 'Aureum') emerges through the ground-covering dicentra, as do the leaves of *Rodgersia aesculifolia*, behind. These are richly bronzed and copper coloured for several weeks in spring before turning green.

RIGHT Hostas flank a path at The Garden House, under mid-summer flowering *Hoheria* 'Glory of Amlwch'. The variegated *Hosta* 'Frances Williams', on the right, tends to scorch in more sunny sites and looks much more healthy and refined in shady conditions.

spring, when the foliage above is at its most dense, such a bed is best left to rest.

Another aspect of maximizing space (left) shows different plants occupying the same piece of ground. This combination at The Garden House in Devon came up year after year. It works as a sustainable planting because the rodgersia's roots are widely spaced, and its top-growth emerges from below ground quite late in the season, thus giving the dicentra a clear, uninterrupted sight of the sky for many weeks before the rodgersia grows up and over it. Although the rodgersia shuts out the light from the dicentra, it makes no difference by this time as the dicentra has already gone dormant. The earlier growth of the dicentra has another advantage in that it helps protect the emerging flower stems of the rodgersia

presence of the water (*left* and *right*). When sunlight is allowed to percolate through the canopy foliage as well, then you may well get something truly memorable. Sunlight (whether filtered or direct), overhanging trees and water, combine to produce an often-overlooked effect of bounced light on to the underside of the trees. It is rather like having a fluid mirror creating constantly shifting and varied light patterns on everything in the vicinity, adding a priceless magical quality.

In this area of Mount Cuba in Delaware (*right*), the quality and balance of light to shade and the inspired planting of the packeras would make this a beautiful area even were the water not there. With water added to the equation, you could sit on the bench and watch the evening sun perform a light show with the shadows, leaves, and water, which would grace heaven itself. It would be an experience to last a lifetime, as long as the mosquitoes are not biting.

Grand country gardens are clearly way beyond the aspirations of most people, but the principles they exhibit and the feelings they evoke are still very relevant to the vast majority with much more humble plots. In essence, the

from minor frosts, cementing a very convenient ground-sharing arrangement.

Water in the garden

If one of your aims in shaded areas of a country garden is to introduce a sense of calm relaxation, then there is nothing like still stretch of water. The tugging of the emotional strings is immeasurably strengthened by the

ABOVE In another part of Mount Cuba, golden ragwort (*Packera aurea*) fulfils the same role as *Primula japonica* (*see opposite*). Large drifts of a single plant in such a big space create a unified, natural looking impression in the area.

water features shown here comprise a stretch of water, narrow and winding in one case and broad in the other, bordered by self-seeding perennials under an overhead canopy of branches. Scaled down for a small shaded area, a miniature version would still work well. Japanese maples or amelanchiers could take the place of the forest trees, and low-growing perennials or woodland alpines could grow alongside the water. In a woodland garden in which you are aiming for calm, a rushing stream would be inappropriate unless you have a steeply sloped garden. A better choice, and considerably less expensive as well as easier to create, would be a pond. With a pond, it would certainly be feasible to produce a similar effect to the stream in another part of Mount Cuba (*left*). The water need not be very deep as it is there as much for its reflective, atmospheric qualities as anything else.

Foliage centre stage

With barely a flower in sight, the Elizabeth Miller Garden in Seattle in late spring (*below* and *right*) proves that there is no need to depend on flowers to create interest in a shady garden. In fact quite the reverse is true. With overhead protection from the potentially scorching sun, foliage comes into its own and is easier to keep looking good for a much greater part of the year than in a sunnier site. It is better therefore to concentrate on foliage shapes, textures, and colours, and to employ flowers in a secondary role in a shady garden.

Although tall, mature trees are present, this part of the Elizabeth Miller Garden is likely to be shaded for only part of the day. Evidence for this would come from the planting to the left

of the path (*right*), which is largely composed of dwarf conifers that would lose their compact habit in too dense a shade. They do, however, contribute to the fairytale, house-in-the-wood atmosphere.

From a purely practical point of view, the conifers also provide an easily maintained border, which will remain green all year, even if it is a little short on flowers. The drama will come from other sources, notably the magnificent cordyline in the pot, and, later in the year, from the autumn colour of the maple and the winter flowers of the witch hazel.

In a more heavily shaded garden than this and on acid soil, evergreen azaleas would fill the role of the conifers, providing domed mounds of greenery which are weed suppressing once established. If low maintenance is important, the bed could be covered in a plastic membrane like black

RIGHT A hardy variety of maidenhair fern (*Adiantum aleuticum*) here grows alongside a path with the black grass-like *Ophiopogon planiscapus* 'Nigrescens'. This ophiopogon is best in half-shade and can be seen again, used with other grasses, on p.116.

ABOVE This section of the Elizabeth Miller Garden is dominated almost entirely by plants chosen for their foliage. If kept healthy, such plants are reasonably maintenance-free and remain fairly constant through the year.

polythene, the shrubs could be planted through it, and the whole area mulched.

The Elizabeth Miller Garden should strictly be called an urban garden, but its scale and size allows it to sneak into the country garden category. It also demonstrates another key country garden feature – the relationship between a garden and its boundaries. In a typical urban garden, the perimeter fences and walls are unavoidably part of almost every view, with the house dominating the design

and being at least partly responsible for the resulting shady conditions.

A shady country garden, by contrast, does not usually have the house in close attendance, and the garden's boundaries, if they are in view, may be of surrounding countryside. With the house out of the picture or at least behind the viewer, any building in the country version is likely to be of the garden retreat or studio type, which is the case with this Seattle garden, thus lending it a more rustic air.

ABOVE Reflecting Dan
Hinkley's passion for
collecting unusual plants,
Heronswood is a
breathtaking assemblage
of unusual plants. It is a
living, breathing reference
library and stands near
the pinnacle of this strand
of gardening.

Two west coast "greats"

Visiting gardens and gleaning ideas from other
people's solutions to shady sites is always
worthwhile. There are many styles of shady
gardens that are open to the public, from
grand display woodland gardens typefied in
the UK by Exbury, in Hampshire, through to
intimate gems such as Bosvigo, the Perrys'
garden, in Cornwall.

The two gardens featured on these pages
would figure highly on anybody's list of great
American woodland gardens. Heronswood

(*above* and on p. 56) is situated near Seattle
in Washington State. It was created by Dan
Hinkley and Robert Jones over a period of
about 15 years and is a truly staggering
collection of shade-loving plants, many
starting life as seeds gathered by Dan from
around the world. There can be few people
on the planet who could match Dan's
encyclopedic knowledge of plants, the weight
of which he carries lightly and with good
humour. His ability to communicate his
expertise is seemingly effortless. In many

ways, his garden mirrors his attributes, with
its simple paths below towering conifers
meandering between borders packed with
a vast range of well-labelled and often rare
plants. Heronswood is truly paradise for all
those fascinated by plants.

The O'Byrnes' garden near Eugene in
Oregon is a masterly artistic creation deserving
widespread recognition. I have been lucky
enough to visit it in both spring and summer.
Each time, I have been "blown away" by the
incredibly detailed, artistic eye of its creators

and the rude health of the plants. The effect
is made all the more amazing because of the
sheer hard work and dedication required to
keep this relatively small, intimate garden
looking this good. With no rain falling in the
summer months, watering becomes a constant
chore. I came home determined not to
complain about summer rainfall ever again.

Growing old gracefully

The commitment needed to create a woodland
garden as good as the O'Byrnes' left me feeling

RIGHT This cleverly
thought-out and beautifully
executed section of a
garden in Vermont will
not require too much
maintenance because the
weeds are squeezed out
by shrubs and vigorous
ground-covering
perennials. It will continue
to look good throughout
the year, despite radically
changing its character.

ABOVE The tall stems of
Cardiocrinum giganteum
hold aloft powerfully
fragrant white flowers in
this half-shady corner of
the UBC Botanical Garden
in Vancouver. The
candelabra primulas and
Rodgersia sambucifolia (in
the foreground) flourish
in permanently damp soil.

decidedly tired. The ageing process should not
be ignored in a garden either, and you should
consider how the garden will look through the
winter. Especially if there are many perennials
present, you should think about whether the
garden will grow old gracefully in autumn.

Some plants, such as conifers and
evergreen shrubs, look pretty much the same
from one month to the next except for brief
periods of flowering or new growth colours,
and these can form the backbone of the
garden. Seasonality comes from deciduous
trees and shrubs, perennials, bulbs, ferns, and
grasses. Of these, tall perennials are the most
likely to strike a discordant note in autumn
unless attention has been paid as to what they
look like as they die back.

Joe Eck and Wayne Winterrowd in their
garden at Northill in Vermont (*right*) have done
a wonderful job balancing summer foliage,

textures, and colour with a dignified decline
into dormancy. Very wisely, in this particular
corner of their garden, tall perennials are
noticeable for their absence.

The particularly common problem in New
England rural areas is also evident here: it is
the lower branches on the conifer trimmed by
deer. Fortunately, in this case, the deer damage
could trigger a change that may improve the
garden still further. It has drawn attention to
the conifer, which might otherwise just be
taken for granted. If those lower damaged
branches were removed entirely, the conifer
trunks would become more noticeably
silhouetted, and there would be a better visual
flow from this immediate part of the garden to
the one on the far side. Autumn is a very good
time to look at trunk and branch silhouettes,
because yellow autumn colour particularly
throws them into sharp relief.

URBAN RETREATS

Parks in any city or town are clearly retreats for millions of urban dwellers, but what I am referring to here are private gardens in built-up areas.

LEFT This small garden is crammed full of plants, many of which grow in containers. Everything about it, from the number of plants to the concrete and pebble spiral design hard-surfacing, suggest that this garden is a calm sanctuary for its owners.

For the vast majority of people, town gardens are typically small, confined spaces that are shaded for at least part of the day by surrounding houses, fences, or trees. These parameters form the framework for the garden picture you might wish to create, whether it be for a lush green oasis, a flower-filled extravaganza, or a simple minimalistic plot.

The depth of shade and the length of time the garden is shaded each day will dictate the style and range of planting. For example, at one extreme, a garden overshadowed by a neighbour's tall conifer trees will not support a flower-bedecked garden, where conditions will limit the range of plants which can be grown. Even in this scenario, instead of bemoaning your apparent bad luck, you could view this situation in a positive frame of mind. By limiting your options away from the "anything is possible, I am spoilt for choice" angle, you can now explore more fully how to be creative in a narrower field. You can

maximize the use of hard surfaces, containers, and filtered and dappled light, as well as adopt a more limited palette of plant material. As with so many other walks of life, necessity can be the mother of invention in garden design.

At the other extreme, a garden with little shade and low fences would not suit a lush green oasis style. Of course if you are of the rebellious school of thought you may wish to kick such generalizations into the next county, but it is undoubtedly true that to buck established guidelines successfully makes life considerably more difficult.

I would suggest you let the design and planting style be initially guided by the primary intended use of the space you have at your disposal and by the physical conditions, such as aspect and climate, and by your garden experiences. This requires some basic observations. In the context of this book, this means noting which parts of the garden are shaded and for how long, what part of each day this occurs, what times of the year, and whether the shaded area under question is dry for part or all of the year.

When space is severely limited, the importance of deciding what above all else is to be the primary purpose of your space cannot be overstressed. Is the garden in effect to serve as an external room, as in several of the examples shown here? Perhaps it might be an extension of the dining area, where you can

enjoy intimate star-lit dinners. Maybe the main requirement for the garden is that it looks good when viewed from within the house at night, when the shading trees can be artfully illuminated, or perhaps it is to provide an attractive area for sitting under shady trees at midday to just "chill". Then again you may just want somewhere to garden, to benefit from the therapy that tending and caring for plants brings with it. Even though these two aspects of gardening are not mutually exclusive, you must decide which is the more important and then let the old adage "form follows function" kick in.

Another "room"

Most people I guess would like their gardens to flow seamlessly from within the house to outside. However, if your objective is to use your exterior space as you would a conservatory, but without its protective roof, then it helps if you can create the illusion of the walls and ceilings of an inside room.

In the wonderful example of Bill Wheeler's garden in New York State (right), you have all the visual elements of a real conservatory with the tree trunks effectively the supporting pillars, and the canopy of the leaning tree substituting for the roof (with built-in shading). Even the low fence has a parallel with the low walls that often underpin the windows in a conservatory. This is more of an external shaded relaxation room than a space for hands-on gardening, other than for the pottering type of jobs one would normally associate with conservatories.

By contrast, Stephen Woodham's small town garden (left) is mainly one for the pursuit of gardening itself, and its rest and relaxation benefits are derived from fussing over the

BELOW This very shady corner of a garden in New York State, where summer sunshine can be relied on, has been brilliantly designed to take account of the hot climate. The thin sections of silhouetted trellis mirror the delicacy of the chairs and emphasize the bright sunshine beyond.

plants themselves. If nothing else, the lack of tables and chairs would suggest this is the garden of a hands-on gardener.

In the Christopher Masson-designed garden (*right*), an exterior "room" atmosphere is again created, but this time without "windows" allowing views away, and also without an overall "roof". The vistas and detailing are all internal, and they are aimed at keeping your interest at eye level or lower. This rich green haven in London includes a smattering of evergreen shrubs spread throughout the design to maintain the effect through the winter months.

In the confined, very still space scents will linger on the air, and shrubs and climbers with scented flowers are well represented. Lilacs, roses, and buddleias flower in early summer, and honeysuckles, wisteria, and mahonias among others contribute at other times of the year. The beautifully constructed shaded bower wreathed in honeysuckle not only provides privacy and a place to sit but also acts as a strong focal point from the house.

Shade providing sanctuary

There is a primitive instinct in humans which makes them feel protected when they are enclosed. Perhaps it has something to do with their perceptions that, with a screen behind them and/or overhead, danger is unlikely to come from those directions.

This feeling of safety induces a sense of calm relaxation, which can be deliberately harnessed by a gardener who places a seat, for example, under the branches of a spreading tree with views out towards the sunshine. I would almost guarantee that even the most slavishly hard-working gardener will while away some hours sitting in such a seat in the

ABOVE In this garden, intricate brickwork is cleverly counter-balanced by plain white walls and the restrained use of bright colour. These factors can be especially relevant in very shady, confined spaces.

shade on a hot summer's day. It is a well-tried tip, and in this chapter all of the gardens that include seats have adopted the same technique to varying degrees.

Another universal feature of these urban gardens is their use of hard surfacing. There is hardly a blade of grassed lawn in any of those illustrated in this chapter. That is not to say a grassed area should not be included, but it does have significant drawbacks especially when the garden is shady. The more shade there is, the greater the problems of maintaining grass in any sort of reasonable state. Grass grows more patchily in shade, therefore becoming muddier in the wet,

which leads on to compaction and as a result even poorer growth.

A more practical form of hard surfacing in a confined shady spot, even when children are part of the equation, would be a wide area of decking (*right*). Being in California, the owner of this garden would welcome shade as there will always be plenty of bright sunshine to look out on from under the shade of that splendid mature magnolia.

By contrast, the lightness of sunshine can be introduced by painting the boundary and house walls white (*as shown above*), and this effect will be noticed even on a dull day. The clean light colour of these walls emphasizes the detailed intricacy of the brickwork and the rich greenery of the plants.

The children factor

With the possible exception of the Californian garden (*below*), my feelings are that the sections of the gardens featured in this chapter are not all that children friendly. This is more of an observation than a criticism, even though I do admit to the notion that children and small plant-filled gardens are not really compatible.

My own son, who is not generally that interested in gardening, may well have liked these featured gardens because in many of them there is a nice quiet seat to read a book, but apart from this pastime and perhaps the pond (*left*) there does not seem to be a lot to keep children occupied.

Since the child is present in all of us, however well buried, some of the same

reasoning can apply in our adult lives. We either want to sit and relax or else play in the garden. Only as adults we are more complicated, and our play is rather more of the weeding and tending plants type than simply kicking a football.

The garden on p.48 is possibly an exception in that it appears to have been designed neither for a plant-lover nor for the benefit of children, although I do not doubt that small children would love to walk up the path to investigate that enticing, fairytale-looking building. This green oasis was designed to be low maintenance. Most direct pleasure from it is gleaned from within the buildings at either end or else from passing through the greenery en route to the very pretty summerhouse. The garden does not seem to be a place to linger in. However, for its primary purpose, which I am sure was to be a

RIGHT Magnolia trees generally do not appreciate heavy wear and tear on ground under which their roots are growing. A clever solution was therefore found to this problem in California, where decking was erected under the canopy of a large magnolia.

LEFT The white painted garden room, statue, and pale-coloured pea gravel on the paths all help to counter-balance the mass of greenery in this restful garden, which needs very little regular maintenance.

RIGHT The functional rather than inspired use of space in this garden is all the more unexpected as it is in San Francisco, where the relatively mild climate and regular summer sunshine means that more adventurous solutions could have been found.

BELOW In a small space, plants can be chosen that create an interesting landscape in miniature. Maidenhair ferns (*Adiantum pedatum*), on their thin, wiry, black stems, rise above foam flower (*Tiarella cordifolia*) and look like a tightly packed copse of trees.

verdant canvas filling the views from the house windows with lush greenery, it succeeds brilliantly, especially with the white-timbered building forming a fabulous focal point.

Urban gardens in sunny climates

Although the gardens featured on p.49 and on the right are situated in sunny climates, there is far more sense of location in the latter. The

BELOW In a small space, plants can be chosen that create an interesting landscape in miniature. Maidenhair ferns (*Adiantum pedatum*), on their thin, wiry, black stems, rise above foam flower (*Tiarella cordifolia*) and look like a tightly packed copse of trees.

garden on p.49 is actually in San Francisco, but it could be situated nearly anywhere in the northern hemisphere where winters are not too harsh. The long, narrow shape is typical of an urban garden. I am sure it provides a very functional space for its owners, who have their privacy protected by the tall pittosporum hedges. However, these same hedges also emphasize the narrowness of the garden.

When viewed from this high angle, my initial thoughts at least would be to explore the removal of the variegated phormium with the strap-shaped leaves, which is growing beyond the seating area, and to think about planting another eucalyptus closer to the house.

The latter, as it very quickly grows up, will afford welcome shade and allow a more tangible sense of a sunny climate and perhaps even create enough privacy in the future to allow for the partial removal of the hedges. The other advantage of another eucalyptus tree planted just beyond the seating area would be that, from the spot the photograph was taken, you would not be able to see all of the garden at once, instantly conjuring up some secrecy and mystery to the garden as a whole.

Elegant and very effective shading can also be created by bamboos, which have been used extensively (right). So fast do these grow in a sheltered urban garden that they have to be chosen carefully. They should be thinned annually of smaller, weaker canes, too.

Planting trees to make shade is not always an option in an urban situation because their height might obscure a neighbour's valued vista or there may simply be insufficient space for a tree to flourish. One way to overcome this difficulty would be to build an arbour or a pergola and train climbing plants to grow over the top of the structure.

RIGHT This patio design has the cool sophistication of an elegant house in a warm climate. The modern-looking chairs match the silver foliage of the central *Astelia chathamica*, and the overhead leaves of banana and tree fern are reminiscent of a ceiling fan in a tropical house.

VERTICAL ELEMENTS

In a limited space or reasonably featureless location the possibilities of introducing vertical elements into a design come more into play.

LEFT This is a beautifully colour-coordinated composition with pink running through the picture, from the pelargonium in the foreground and *Geranium maderense* behind to the brickwork and terracotta pots. Blue-mauve colouring appears on the sleeper risers and in the wisteria flowers.

Employing vertical features of interest such as a pergola or arbour can double the value of a given space. You can have flowers and interest spilling over the top of the pergola, while a whole different planting scheme occurs at ground level. Such vertical elements also provide clean architectural lines, shade, and strong shadows.

I love them as well for the shapes created in the carpentry and for that sense of protected sanctuary touched on in the "Urban Retreats" chapter (pp.40–51), especially when the border on one side is heavily planted and the other is open with views into the garden. Some pergolas almost conjure the atmosphere of a section of cloister (left). Perhaps, best of all, pergolas and arbours give you an opportunity to grow wisteria in a way that best displays its incredible beauty.

On a purely practical note, I do wonder how easy it will be to access this wisteria for pruning purposes as the cross-timbers of the pergola are so closely spaced. However the owners of this garden manage it, they have quite obviously succeeded.

I personally prefer the top cross-timbers on a pergola to be wider spaced, at least 1m (3ft) apart, so it becomes easier to train the long shoots of the climbing plants to them. More importantly, the greater spacing enables the sun to send shafts of light through to the ground, creating strong shadows.

Pergola variation

An unusual adaptation of a pergola has been employed in Karla Newell's garden in Brighton in southern England (*see p.55*). Here the timberwork appears to have a pitch almost as in a building which has not then been roofed. From the exposed "rafters" a whole series of hanging baskets, lights, and ornaments are then hung, which coupled with containers standing on the ground provides colour and interest on a range of different levels. I love it.

LEFT The regularly spaced shaggy trunks of river birch form strong vertical lines in this contemporary fusion of eastern and western gardening styles. The weathered timber channels the eye and provides a practical boundary between moss and pebbles.

RIGHT An exciting blend of pitched structural timbers, trelliswork, and brightly coloured walls in Karla Newell's garden gives this narrow space an added dimension, creating a garden in the air. If desired, the ground can be kept largely clear.

This would be an excellent way of treating those often quite narrow spaces running alongside the house.

Using tree trunks

A very different vertical element is introduced into the very elegant and simple garden (left), which has a distinct oriental feel. The strong vertical element to the design is carried through primarily by the shaggy trunks of the river birch (*Betula nigra*), and in a more minor role by the framework of the windows and the stems of the bamboos to the right. By spacing the trees at fairly regular intervals, the designers have also linked them to the evenly spaced uprights in the building and fences, thus contributing to the unity of the overall composition. Incidentally, I could just have

ABOVE These mock classical columns surrounding a pond in Heronswood perfectly complement the vertical trunks of the sheltering conifers. Contrast is provided by the *Cornus controversa* 'Variegata', sometimes called the wedding cake tree because of its strongly horizontal branching, which is planted close by.

easily described this garden in the "Hard Landscaping" chapter (*pp.*60–9) to show how dramatic weather-worn timber can look when used in flat planks.

At Heronswood in Washington State, mock classical columns (*above*) provide an attractive and clever surround to a delightful circular pond. These columns break up the uniformity and sameness that are a potential problem in a woodland garden. In the process of pushing above the jungle-like, lush foliage, these columns achieve on a more intimate scale

what the ramrod-straight trunks of the Douglas firs are doing to the understorey of the garden generally.

In another part of this garden, similar vertical columns are again employed, this time acting as plant stands for large containers filled with foliage plants. At up to 3m (10ft) high, these columns also serve as a conduit to screen the water pipes that run up through them and are used for watering the containers, making this task a much simpler operation than it otherwise would be.

BELOW Occasionally, the design of a garden is enhanced by a well-composed picture of it. Here, for example, the horizontal lines of the stonework show particularly well against the vertical plant stems when seen through the viewfinder of a camera.

Vertical uprights on a small scale

One of the most effective uses of vertical sculpture I have seen was in a shaded bed between two wings of a house, the side walls being partly obscured by the addition of about two dozen ceramic "poles". These were buff and cream in colour, about 5cm (2in) in diameter and up to 2m (6½ft) in height. When seen against the plum-red shingles cladding the wall, the glossy green leaves of asarums and disporums, the golden-foliaged grasses, and the rich red-brown bark mulch, this bed oozed sophisticated coolth.

On a much smaller scale, these same strong vertical elements can be easily created in any garden. The hellebores (*below*) appear to be growing near the margins of the romantic setting of an old vineyard. The more mundane truth, which is however much more achievable, is that they are in fact thriving beneath the pruned stems of common buddleias. It just goes to show that beauty can take many forms, and often you just need to look much more closely to find it.

By cutting the buddleias back hard each spring to 45–60cm (18–24in) high, and by cutting out entirely any small branches below this height, you will enable light to reach the hellebores just at flowering time. They will then be able to make their growth before the

LEFT This hawthorn hedge has been immaculately laid and incorporated into a Chelsea Flower Show exhibit. Layering like this takes considerable skill and patience but would reward the practitioner with a living partition which looks almost better with no foliage in winter than when it is in full leafy growth.

RIGHT A screen that has been very cleverly made of ordinary bamboo canes looks just right behind this bed of mostly ferns. The cut-off stubs of the old leaves on the tree fern trunk match the pattern and density of the fence behind. The black-stemmed fern in the foreground is *Dryopteris wallichiana*.

garden. When orientated on an east–west axis there will clearly be a sunny side and a shady one, instantly creating a surprising amount of shade and shelter. Two examples of fences are illustrated here: a living one (*left*) and a more conventional one (*right*). The living laid hedge is particularly valuable as a boundary line in exposed, windy locations where external views are important, because unlike a fence it will not get blown over. Other styles of fence are shown on pp. 47, 63, 94, 114, 118, and 124. They all impart a different mood and varying degrees of transparency.

I particularly like the ingenuity of the bamboo fence made with standard bamboo canes (*right*). Canes of greater diameter than this are difficult to come by in the UK, which is a shame as larger-diametered versions contribute so much to oriental gardens. Still, this version in an English garden has exciting possibilities, perhaps on a smaller scale with 1.2m (4ft) canes and with panels zigzagging between woodland plants.

In this bamboo fence, there are sufficient gaps between the canes to allow clematis to twine around them, enabling it to become a patchwork of foliage, flowers, and ochre-coloured canes later in the season.

buddleias develop enough to reduce the light significantly. Other spring stalwarts such as primroses and pulmonarias will also thrive in a similar situation, as well as bulbs such as scillas, chionodoxas, and wood anemones.

Fences as vertical elements

Fences are clearly important elements of boundary lines, but they are just as important in dividing up internal spaces within the

HARD LANDSCAPING

Gardening in shade will almost certainly require the use of hard landscaping, if for no other reason than grass paths are impractical in such conditions.

How much hard landscaping you use will depend on how dark and dense the shading is in your site, and to an extent on your tastes and the garden style employed. A woodland naturalistic style would benefit from paths and other non-plant material looking as if they might actually occur in some wood or woodland glade somewhere in the wild.

Frank Cabot has achieved this effect at Les Quatre Vents (*left*), where this log path is reminiscent of some remote mountain forest trail and therefore blends perfectly with the woodland plants along its edge. I hope this path is mostly intended for decorative purposes, as it must be potentially lethal for the elderly or in wet weather. More practical and equally effective at providing the "trail" look is to lay a path of bark (*see p.69*).

As you are designing a garden, not a woodland, you are not slavishly bound by this principle of a naturalistic woodland look. Moreover, the intrusion of the ultra-modern in an otherwise traditional woodland garden can be extremely dramatic. Personally I am very comfortable with modern sculpture, for example, but prefer it still to have a strong organic shape even if made of very state-of-the-art materials.

The blending of the modern

The landscape designer Christopher Bradley-Hole turns this concept on its head by producing naturalistic planting combinations within the framework of modern minimalistic simplicity. He does this superbly (*see p.118*).

On a small scale, this technique is arguably more successful in an urban garden that has straight-edged boundaries than in the more diffuse setting of small country gardens. In larger country gardens the style works very well, as Christopher has proved on many occasions by apportioning an area of formality particularly around the house, where straight or formal lines are appropriate.

LEFT Weathered wooden logs create a very natural-looking woodland path in Frank Cabot's garden in Quebec. The problem with wooden paths of any sort in shady conditions, however, is that they can become very slippery.

BELOW Tree stumps can be very effective as focal points, especially in shady locations. Surrounded by a mulch of bark and a few strategically placed ferns, tree stumps can imbue a sense of age and naturalness to nearly any shady spot. As well as looking good in such sites, old stumps also serve a useful purpose because they provide a winter refuge for local wildlife, such as toads and frogs.

If you wish to modernize or revamp parts of an existing shady garden, you might want to consider using modern materials or techniques to produce an up-to-date "take" on an old idea. The sculpture of a swarm of huge flying insects emanating from the ominous depths of the driftwood (left) has a distinct and slightly scary contemporary feel and would probably have given me a minor heart attack if I had bent down to study the driftwood without having first noticed them. The narrow ceramic poles (see p.57) also come into this category, with traditional woodland shade planting taken to a new higher plain by their addition.

Every last construction detail in this tea garden (below) at Hidenin in Kyoto, Japan, complies with the history and tradition of this form of gardening. However, its designer is also very keen to update the style using modern and local materials, and in this garden he has done so with the addition of the beautiful fence in the background. The vertical lines in this barrier are created by using white-coloured canes that give the impression of sunlight filtering through the fence.

More inspiration from the East

You do not have to make a Japanese garden to draw inspiration from the Chinese/Japanese gardening style, and in particular their clever and detailed use of hard landscaping. The principles they espouse are just as relevant in our western gardens, and if modified to the varying climates and gardening aspirations of the West can produce very powerful and distinct western/oriental hybrids.

I have always tried, sometimes subconciously, to incorporate eastern principles of shape and form into my own gardens, but there are others like Robin

RIGHT In this tea garden designed by Marc Peter Keane in Kyoto, the stones and rocks are used traditionally, yet the fence in the background has a more contemporary feel. Its pale upright struts particularly give the illusion of sunlight streaming through the fence.

BELOW This beautifully simple Californian garden is wonderfully in harmony with its surroundings. The twisted trunks of the native trees contrast strongly with the clean lines of the building. Their natural contours are further enhanced by the curving line of the stepping stones and by the use of a limited range of plants.

BELOW Hard landscaping is the dominant feature in this Japanese-style garden constructed for the Chelsea Flower Show, in London. The planting is cast in a supporting role to emphasize the carefully placed rocks, flat stone bridges, and "dry" water feature. The texture, forms, and colours of the plants are muted to help foster the image of background vegetation in a much larger landscape.

Hopper from British Colombia who more actively seeks this fusion of gardening styles. All three of the gardens shown on pp.64–6 have eastern origins, of which only the Chelsea Flower Show exhibit (*see p.65*) is consciously modelled along strict Japanese guidelines.

The clear eastern influence in the Californian garden (*see p.64*) is evident in many of its features, not least in the way the simple stepping stones chart an erratic course through the grass-like planting. This is an extremely effective way of channeling feet on heavy-usage "desire lines" through grassed areas, especially those in shade, where compaction and bare patches would rapidly develop from wear and tear. I have used this technique many times, and it is amazing how most people will conscientiously tread only on the slabs, avoiding the gaps, when faced with stepping stones.

Japanese garden designers are past masters at using hard landscaping to create the essence

LEFT This sophisticated water and rock combination forms part of an unexpectedly subtle design within the Keukenhof gardens in The Netherlands, which is famed for its massed displays of spring bulbs.

BELOW The mossy saxifrages are well named as they do indeed resemble moss when not flowering. They can be substituted for moss in gardens where birds are not too prone to scratching plants in search of food. Here, the saxifrages nestle very effectively among the water-worn rounded pebbles and rocks.

of a wild landscape, and the Chelsea exhibit (*see p.65*) has incorporated many of them, from the rocks and bridges to decking and chippings. All of these tools of the designers' trade, along with water, are just as effective in a more heavily shaded location, but it is worth noting that it is the shafts of sunshine piercing the shadows that bring this photograph to life.

Using water

Water can bring magic to any garden, and its use is not confined to purely sunny gardens. In fact, to my mind dappled light in semi-shady spots is the best place for magic dust to be sprinkled to produce a water feature. Think of summer walks along shaded stream banks with shafts of sunlight reflecting off the water, and you will see what I mean.

Perhaps not many people can stretch to a large pond or even a water flow as large as that at Keukenhof gardens (*left*), but in all other

respects this sort of layout with its mixture of rocks, flat stones, and water-rounded pebbles is very achievable in a shaded garden. The atmosphere in this corner of the gardens is calm and relaxing, mainly due to the foliage colours being limited to shades of green.

Even the smallest spaces can benefit from a water feature, such as the water basin in the Kyoto tea garden (*see p.63*), although in that instance the feature is included for symbolic cleansing of the hands and mouth rather than for aesthetic reasons. I have seen a large Ali-Baba pot used as a pond in a small garden, complete with fish and lotus plant, and it looked superb. With modification, it would have fitted into nearly any garden.

Provided it is in scale with its surroundings, even a tiny water feature could be made to work in one of those very awkward dry, shady locations which seem so problematic. By concentrating on hard landscaping of various

types in such a spot and by using a restricted range of plants which will cope with these conditions, you can turn what was a virtual shady desert into an exciting tiny oasis. If necessary, you may need to grow some plants in containers.

In these awkward shady areas, you could possibly borrow from the Japanese again, where the philosophy of "less is more" is practised in their tea gardens. It is the principle of allowing a tiny amount of colour into the garden, thereby concentrating the visitor's mind on it, and in the process accentuating its importance and relevance. Such a concept is sometimes hard for westerners to grasp, living as they do amid a culture in which excess is the norm. However, the idea has some merit.

It is worth thinking about using only limited bright colour, or perhaps some plant with an exceptional leaf form, and surrounding it with relative simplicity – plants or otherwise – to draw attention to it. Some of the reasons that moss, for example, is very much admired in eastern gardens is because it is interestingly textured, evergreen, and coloured rich green. It can mound itself up in places, creating its own detailed landscape in miniature, and yet it sets off anything it surrounds. I love moss and would use it all the time if only the blackbirds would not revel in scratching it into oblivion.

Mossy saxifrages are rather less prone to this scratching problem, yet still give a "moss" effect and look particularly good growing in the spaces between boulders or rocks. When used in conjunction with pea gravel (*see p.67*), the mossy saxifrage helps to establish a very natural vignette. Alternatively, this type of gravel looks good with grasses (*left*), even if in this instance the design includes rather too many different grasses and is thus over elaborate. A better balance would be achieved if fewer grass types and a rounded rock or two had been used.

Mulching with bark

Because it comprises almost anything that is not actually a plant, hard landscaping has many guises. I will touch on some of them in other chapters, but one mulching material – bark – is obviously more applicable in a woodland garden than anywhere else. It is a medium which triggers quite violent reactions from some quarters of the gardening community who rather look down their noses at its use. However, I think this has probably rather more to do with its overuse in sometimes unsuitable situations.

Woodland is the appropriate place for a bark mulch. If different sizes and colours were readily available, the shade gardener would be able to create seriously interesting possibilities, especially if bark was combined with driftwood or old tree stumps. When used correctly (*right*), it can look just perfect.

BELOW Grasses in a range of foliage colours surrounded by reflective pea shingle form a low-maintenance planting scheme. In this instance, the "blue" grasses and silver-leaved plants would need full sun to thrive, but a mix of brown and golden grasses would survive in shade.

BELOW A very natural and sympathetically coloured mulch covers both the bed and the path leading into the wood. Forget-me-nots, foxgloves, and white-flowered foam flowers, all ecologically in their correct environment, help cement this woodland-edge scene. In the foreground, upright spikes of *Persicaria bistorta* 'Superba' echo the shape and colour of the foxgloves, with iris matching the blue of the forget-me-not flowers.

PLANTS FOR
SHADY GARDENS

SHADY PLANTS IN NATURE

The vast majority of shady plants in nature will flower in spring, taking advantage of the sunlight before the leaves appear on the trees above.

PREVIOUS PAGES
International harmony presides over this Sussex garden where a Japanese maple forms a majestic backdrop to orange Ghent azaleas, which were mainly developed in the early 1800s in Belgium. A carpet of English bluebells completes this natural-looking composition.

LEFT Surely no one who has ever experienced the sights and smell of a bluebell wood will easily forget the moment. Such wonderful sights as this beech wood in Kent are almost taken for granted, yet they are very specific to countries bordering the Atlantic coastline in north-west Europe.

A woodland setting is often a very suitable place for good plant growth, as there is wind protection from the trees and the sun's warmth is concentrated in the humus-rich leaf mould litter covering the ground. This nutrient-rich layer, which is replenished each autumn, is manna from heaven for shade plants and helps to retain moisture. The tree roots suck away any excess. For plant opportunists able to capitalize on this windfall before the tree roots really get to work later in the year and percolate every square centimetre, this is a moment to seize for optimum growing conditions.

Those plants that do start into growth under such conditions increase prolifically, when happy, to produce some of nature's most spectacular floral displays. Think here of bluebells in Europe or wake robins in America. Massed displays although wonderful when they do occur are not, however, the norm among shady plants in nature.

Spring ephemerals

Plants that go through their above-ground phases of growth cycle in the early months of the year, before sitting out the hot summer as seeds or by resting below ground, can be categorized as "spring ephemerals". Most of these spring ephemerals do not create huge pools of colour in the wild, and their individual beauty is less of the in-your-face brash sort and more of the type that benefits from detailed inspection. You need to look closely at the flowers of many woodland plants to spot their poise and exquisite detailing.

In fact, woodland plants from areas of the world where they experience persistent heavy rainfall in their native haunts often have flowers which only ever face the ground, so the outer sepals and petals can act like umbrellas to protect the all-important reproductive organs. Both the botanist in the wild and the gardener growing these plants in his or her garden may discover part

garden. In this summer-shady spot, the grass grew only sparsely and it seemed an ideal location to grow a lot more spring flowers. I planted natives such as primroses, lenten daffodils, early purple orchids, and small patches of blue and white wood anemones, as well as self-seeding exotics such as *Crocus tommasinianus* and, at the far end, Spanish bluebells. I also began scattering large amounts of seed of the North American pink fawn lily (*Erythronium revolutum*), which has since spread to cover half of this area with its pink, Chinese lantern-like flowers. Having introduced so many plants, I clearly wanted them to thrive, so I raised the canopy of the shading lime trees still further to let more spring sunshine reach the ground and aid flowering.

The problem then potentially arises of the grass starting to grow more vigorously and, since it should not be cut until early summer, of swamping the plants you have worked so hard to put there. The answer came with a winter application of a growth retardant, maleic hydrazide or mefluidide, sprayed before any of the bulbs emerged. This single application stopped the grass growing for about three months, which is just long enough to let the spring ephemerals grow, flower, and seed. The growth retardant worked so well that the whole area in the spring months is now covered in a continually changing carpet of flowers, although the celandines – to the pleasure of some and the sadness of others – have been increasingly squeezed out.

Even though this spray is just about the only one I use, I realize that using any chemical at all will offend some people. I mention it because I am asked so often how to grow flowers in grass. The normal routes for growing wildflowers in grass would be either

ABOVE Dutchman's breeches (*Dicentra cucullaria*) flourishes in the Maryland woods on the eastern seaboard of the USA, where it reaches only a few centimetres/inches high. In the same habitat grows the similar *D. canadensis*, also with white flowers.

of the whole charm and enjoyment of shade plants is being able to turn their flowers carefully in order to look into their faces.

Naturalizing flowers in grass

At The Garden House in Devon, celandines (*Ranunculus ficaria*) were growing on the edge of a field, which at the time of this photograph (right) had recently been included within the

RIGHT Celandines take advantage of the thin grass to carpet the ground at The Garden House in Devon. Many other bulbs, including wood anemones, crocuses, erythroniums, and scillas, have since established and naturalized here.

RIGHT Primroses and chionodoxa mingle together at the base of a large magnolia tree. This particular grouping inspired me to plant a grove of magnolias very close together and to grow bulbs and other woodlanders beneath them (*see also p.91*).

ABOVE Although spring-flowering *Triteleia ixioides* seems to prefer half-shade in its native homeland of California, this bulbous plant needs almost full sun in more temperate climates, perhaps to ensure it gets an adequate summer baking.

to plough and reseed; or to strip the topsoil, cultivate, and reseed. Neither of these is practicable in this situation without serious damage to the lime tree roots. My growth retardant is applied at a quiet time of year for wildlife, is a compromise, and wherever it has been used in the garden the number of native species, both fauna and flora, have increased. It is not a solution for everyone, for sure, but it can prove really good for some gardeners.

Primroses

These herald the spring perhaps more than any other native plant and are very amenable as to where they will grow. Where I grew up in north Somerset they were almost exclusively only found growing on the shady side of hedgerows, but in wetter parts of the UK, as in the south-west, they are just as happy in more open, sunnier sites.

Such versatility allows you as a gardener to create natural-looking plantings with non-natives added to a primrose "base". This is exactly what happened at The Garden House (*right*), where primroses and *Chionodoxa sardensis* self-seed around the base of a magnolia tree. A few weeks later, wood anemones and white *Chionodoxa luciliae* Gigantea Group occupy almost the same position, bringing a blue-and-white colour combination into play.

Magnolias really do not like root disturbance, and one expert plantsman I knew even banished heavy stones from the ground where magnolia roots might be in case the weight damaged them. Such vulnerability is worth bearing in mind should you wish to plant beneath an established magnolia. Very limited physical planting should therefore be done, and you should instead rely on the plants spreading naturally by self-seeding.

BELOW Wild lent
daffodils (*Narcissus
pseudonarcissus*) are the
perfect size for mixing
with wood anemones,
although they can be a
bit shy-flowering. Other
dwarf daffodils, such as
the cyclamineus hybrids,
are more reliable and of
similar size.

In another part of the garden I planted a copse of 20 or so magnolias very close together (*see p.91*) to try to recreate and further embellish the spring flower mix (*see p.77*). Because it would be extremely difficult to plant anything when the magnolias grew up, I made sure that the wood anemones, epimediums, primroses, and many spring bulbs were introduced before the magnolias' roots infiltrated the whole bed. After this initial planting period there has been no more soil disturbance. Apart from clearing off the magnolia leaves in autumn, topdressing with a mulch of composted leaf mould at the same time, and periodically removing the lowest magnolia branches to enable sufficient light to reach the ground, the whole area is left to fend for itself. I am delighted to say that it has improved wonderfully year on year.

The area where these primroses were photographed at The Garden House is completely and heavily shaded in summer, but in another area of this same garden primroses are part of a much more intricate plant tapestry in a less shady location (*see p.108*). This is possible because of the usually heavy rainfall (about 1,500mm/60in per annum) in that part of Devon.

In much drier climates such as in California or much of the Mediterranean, shade planting is a completely different ball game. Among scores of other examples I have seen in full shade are agapanthus growing and flowering happily in Italy, schizostylis in South Africa, and tritelia in California, all of which gardeners in the UK would consider to be cast-iron, full-sun candidates. It goes to show therefore that it might be worth experimenting with more supposedly sun-loving plants in shady spots. It is also important to be less dogmatic in your planting schemes and to be more aware of other people's gardening experiences, as unlikely connections might just lead to exciting creative possibilities for your own situations.

Snowdrops

Nobody could fail to be impressed by a display of snowdrops as phenomenal as that at the

ABOVE This wonderful
display of snowdrops
develops in the Painswick
Rococo garden in
Gloucestershire in late
winter. It would be very
feasible to plant other
bulbs in the gaps between
the snowdrops so they
flower later in the spring
and extend the period of
interest in this woodland.

Painswick Rococo garden (*above*). Although
they are of a native species, it is not often that
such snowdrops will create a spectacle like this
in the wild. Competing plants in this garden
setting are almost certainly manually removed
from the snowdrop grove, so nothing spoils
the uninterrupted drifts of white flowers.

Because plants in the wild have to compete
for light, water, and nutrients without the aid
of human gardeners, it is unusual for
herbaceous plants growing there to develop in
large solid groups. Those that do manage to
achieve this supremacy tend to have either

thug-like tendencies, such as bluebells, or
an effective growth strategy such as rapidly
growing, upright stems followed by a
horizontal spreading of often larger leaves
that will block out competition.

Such is the general growth habit of many
woodland wildflowers, and there are lessons
to be learnt for the gardener by looking a little
closer at how such plants adapt to these
conditions. A favourite flower of American
woodlands is wake robin (*Trillium*) (*see p. 141*),
which appears to be quite frail on first
inspection, but once it has unfurled its ruffs

of broad leaves its ability to collar all available light is pretty productive. Such efficiency occasionally translates into impressive natural stands of wake robins carpeting the woods. Although the leaves are extremely good at catching light, they are relatively thin-textured and are consequently easily damaged by wind, so in my experience what they do not like is a draughty spot in the garden.

Virginian bluebells (*Mertensia virginica*) grow in the same type of open woodlands as wake robins (*Trillium* species) in Maryland. Although

LEFT A wonderfully natural effect has been created in these deciduous woodlands at Redfield Wildflower Garden in Connecticut. White dicentras, pink primulas, and yellow poppies stud the green carpet of low-growing, shade-loving perennials and ferns. In the middle distance, sumptuous patches of colour are provided by the woodland phlox.

RIGHT Although the vast majority of Virginian bluebells are blue flowered, there are occasional pink- and white-flowered specimens such as these ones growing here in some woods in Maryland.

Virginian bluebells (*above*) may not produce as dense a floral display as English bluebells do in the UK, they can give large sections of woods a subtle, clear blue wash and are very beautiful.

To a European eye, a more direct visual comparison with English bluebells is given by the quamash (*Camassia quamash*). In the Pacific north-west I saw it producing almost exactly the same floral effect in similar growing conditions to those enjoyed by English bluebells. However, as the Pacific north-west experiences drier summers than the UK, quamash is likely to do better in drier conditions than English bluebells prefer.

Therefore, if you are contemplating a meadow garden, maybe in an orchard, and would like a "wash" of a good clean blue, up to 45cm (18in) high, you should consider using quamash. Its bulbs are almost as inexpensive as those of bluebells and may establish better in grass in half-shade.

Another feature of the Maryland floodplain (*above*) is how the individual grace and form of the two main protagonists in this woodland are lost when seen en masse. Both Virginian bluebells and ostrich fern (*Matteuccia struthiopteris*) exhibit the same growth pattern as wake robin, of growing up and then out to catch the light, although Virginian bluebells — as I know from personal experience — are not as good at coping with anti-social neighbours as either of the other two plants.

Ostrich fern is often called shuttlecock fern, for obvious reasons when you see the individual crowns. This exceptionally tough and resilient fern spreads rapidly by underground runners when settled, so be warned but not put off. It is a really beautiful and easy fern to cultivate, and the garden benefits visually if the number of fern crowns are thinned periodically.

Evening inspiration

Ideas can be gleaned from nature in some of the most unexpected circumstances, and I was certainly not looking for garden inspiration in Oregon when I was searching for erythroniums in flower. However, by the time I came across this patch of *Erythronium citrinum* (*below*), the sun had sunk quite low and was flooding everything with a glorious golden glow that only an evening sun can bestow.

The erythroniums were growing on top of a bank under manzanita (*Arctostaphylos*) bushes whose trunks were polished mahogany in colour — much the same shade as the rocks scattered round about. Older erythronium flowers were tinged with pink, and this was exactly the same colour combination as that of the manzanita's flowers a metre above. It all added up to a memory I shall never forget. It is a grouping I am now trying to recreate in my own garden, substituting *Rhododendron glaucophyllum* with its copper-coloured trunks for the more difficult to grow manzanita. The rhododendron has the same open growth habit and similar-sized leaves but is much easier to cultivate in the wetter UK climate.

RIGHT *Erythronium citrinum* takes advantage of the cooler conditions to be found beneath manzanita bushes so it is able to carpet the ground in the Illinois valley in southern Oregon.

Weaving patterns of colour

Because solid blocks of a single species are not the norm in wild woodland conditions, as mentioned earlier in this chapter, the purple-blue wild phlox (*right*) when growing in large groups may thread a random pattern around the edges, as it has here through a carpet of white-fringed phacelia. From a gardener's viewpoint, this diffuse arrangement is far more subtle and pleasing to the eye than if these same two plants were grouped in solid blocks of the same colour. It is undoubtedly a very beautiful combination that I would be delighted to have gracing my garden.

However, were it mine and space was limited, I think I might try and add a few slightly taller plants from another genus to bring a different texture, form, and flower colour towards the top left of this particular view. Something perhaps like *Tiarella wherryi* (*left*) would work, if its flowering time coincided. If space is not an issue, the simplicity of leaving two complementary colours to produce a patchwork over a large area can be jaw-droppingly good, as can be seen in the middle distance of the woodland garden on p.80.

This effect is one I try to employ as often as I can in all parts of my own garden, with generally one type of plant weaving in and out of many of its neighbours, blending and harmonizing the whole composition. When it works and it can be just as effective with foliage alone, this sort of grouping appears very natural wherever it is sited. Although large groupings are obviously very memorable, I still try to follow these blending guidelines when planting tiny areas of just a square metre (square yard) with alpines or bulbs, so fundamental is this planting philosophy to me.

ABOVE *Tiarella wherryi* is native to the woods of the south-eastern states of America. With its dark flowering stems, pink buds, and veined and slightly marbled leaves, it is one of the more elegant and colourful species of foam flower.

RIGHT The white-fringed phacelia *Phacelia fimbriata* blends attractively with wild blue phlox (*Phlox divaricata*). Both are natives of the woods in eastern USA.

CREATING SHADE

To a plant lover like myself, woodland shade-loving plants are so desirable that I attempt to create suitable shaded areas if none exists in a garden.

LEFT The open branchwork and trunk structure of the flowering dogwoods (this is *Cornus kousa*) lend themselves to selective pruning to allow cultivation of shade-loving plants below. As with magnolias, once the dogwood has been planted the ground should not be dug to protect the dogwood's roots.

There are a number of ways that a shaded site suitable for woodlanders can be created and still look as if it were a natural part of the garden. These include using existing plantings, making a mini wood, and erecting a pergola or other vertical structure such as a windbreak.

The most obvious method is to provide shady areas under existing trees and shrubs. You may indeed have some shrubs that have been growing for several years, so long in fact that you hardly notice their presence from one year to the next. Alternatively, you may have an individual shrub clothed with branches to the ground or possibly a whole group that has grown together. In the latter case, moving or scrapping a few of the perimeter shrubs, which are always the most leafy, may suddenly open up the whole group. It may then be possible to treat the remaining shrubs as a single unit, as if it were a copse in its own right. By removing their dead, crossing, and internal branches with no access to the canopy,

you can form an interesting "wood" even before any shade-loving plants are introduced.

Selectively removing branches

Cutting off lower branches on shrubs can open up a previously unused piece of real estate, as has already been seen on pp. 29 and 57. Nor do you have to remove all of the lower branches. I have often found it to be very successful if the branches on one side only are taken out. For example, in this dogwood tree (*left*) you could take off the lower course of smaller branches entirely, up to a height of about 1m (3ft), to create potential planting spaces below. Alternatively, you could remove only the lower branches on the far side, thereby retaining the fullness of the shrub when viewed from the lawn and still giving you almost as much planting space beneath when accessed from the rear. From the front viewpoint, it also retains the secrecy and mystery element engendered by not being able to see all of the garden at once.

ABOVE Many pieris
develop very handsome
trunks as they get older
with flaking, chestnut-
coloured bark that almost
rivals paperbark maple
(*Acer griseum*). By
selectively removing
the lower branches,
this *Pieris* 'Firecrest'
has been opened up
and transformed into
a specimen in its
own right.

One of the keys to achieving this successfully is to chose your "trees" carefully. In fact, if space is limited the plants need not be trees at all but shrubs that have a tree-like look to them, such as the Japanese maple (*right*). Several of the same type of "tree" planted in the same area will successfully create a "wood" with half-shady conditions beneath.

The whole process of planting your own shady woodland for immediate effect can be scaled up by however much you want. If available space is not a restricting factor, a copse of widely spaced birch trees would do the job just as effectively (*see p.54*) and allow bigger woodland plants to be grown beneath. This is the ploy so often employed by flower show exhibitors wishing to bring the illusion of woodland to their designs.

This recently pruned pieris (*above*) is another, perhaps less obvious, example of this same process. As a result of selective branch removal, an interesting feature has been created as well as planting spaces where none existed before. You are in effect turning shrubs into small specimen trees. Such a technique works on a very wide range of shrubs from azaleas, rhododendrons, camellias, pieris, viburnums, and dogwoods to conifers of many sorts.

Remember you cannot stick branches back on again, so take your time when pruning. A further branch can always come off later when you have had time living with the new shape.

Plant your own mini woodland

Another solution if you do not have any woodland conditions is to plant your own mini woodland. This does not take anywhere near as long as you might think, and it is possible to create suitable conditions over the course of a weekend.

Beds under vertical features

It would also be possible to provide shade with the aid of man-made structures. The area beneath vertical elements such as pergolas can prove a very desirable planting location. By eliminating the traditional path under a pergola, you could take this idea a stage further and erect a pergola under which there is a continuous planted bed. It would make a very nice feature and focal point.

Taken one step further again, the whole of a small garden could be covered by a canopy with woodland beds beneath. I can imagine this being possible in an urban front garden where part of this overhead construction is used to shelter the car. It would be like an extended carport with a garden alongside.

Windy gardens

Ways of introducing shade on to a windy site are not always straightforward. A problem

I had in my current garden, when it was an open field, was that any tree or shrub planted to create shade was blasted by the wind, as would have been anything planted beneath. This kind of windy location is not ideal, or even vaguely acceptable to more high-brow woodlanders.

Strong windbreak fences would solve the problem with shading stretched horizontally above head height to provide shelter. Such a solution would be functional, but no one could pretend that it was very pretty.

I personally tried to solve this problem by physically landscaping the ground into mini hills and valleys up to 3m (10ft) in height. In effect, these raised beds then had a sunny side and, more pertinently, a shady side as well. Then, even relatively small shrubs and trees planted on the tops of these hills cast long shadows, and the woodland plants have the benefit of sheltering in its shade as well as the leeward protection of the hill itself. In such an environment they have thrived.

ABOVE When trained as a multi-trunked half-standard, Japanese wisteria (*Wisteria floribunda*) looks good flowering above perennials, such as daylilies, as well as ferns.

Lower-growing spring-flowering bulbs and woodlanders are even better in this situation, giving the wisteria's trunks more prominence.

RIGHT Magnolias were deliberately close-planted, and multi-trunking encouraged, at The Garden House in Devon, to increase the "natural" feel of these areas. Underneath, pink fawn lily (*Erythronium revolutum*) flourishes alongside white- and blue-flowered wood anemones and other spring bulbs in the undisturbed soil.

PLANTING IN SHADE

How do you proceed once you have created a shady spot or identified which part of the existing impenetrable gloom you would like to turn into garden?

LEFT This raised bed provides a home for a well-composed collection of foliage plants. Even in winter the rhododendron (top right), silver-variegated euonymus, and ivy sprawling on to the wall behind will still hold interest. However, the containerized *Astelia chathamica* 'Silver Spear' will need taking indoors.

The first thought you need to grasp is that the actual physical shading, that is, the diminished light caused by overhead obstructions of any sort, is only a relatively small part of the equation in successful cultivation of woodland plants. Physical shading can often be modified fairly easily, or if this is not feasible then it can be catered for in your planning. What is much more important are the conditions under and at ground level.

Although you may believe that you now have half-shady conditions which should be perfect for woodlanders, this may not prove to be the case until you have prepared the ground properly. How thoroughly you do this depends on what you want to grow. If you are going to use plants chosen from lists for their ease of cultivation and do not wish to "fuss" over the bed too much in future, then you need only make sure that the area is forked over with a garden fork and cleared of tough perennial weeds.

Preparing for treasures

Alternatively, you may want to fill your shade bed with treasures such as wake robins, orchids, or unusual epimediums. These very desirable plants tend to be much slower to increase so are easily overrun by more vigorous neighbours. They are therefore best suited to a bed of their own where they can be given a little more tender care.

If you have chosen such plants for the new bed, then you should dig the ground as deeply as you can to remove all roots, living or dead. Add as much garden compost and leaf mould as you are able to lay your hands on, as well as coarse grit if you want. If your conscience allows, dig in some peat as well, because it helps to make the ground more spongy. You are aiming for a loose, open medium that can ideally be almost planted with your bare hands, and without a trowel. Once this has been achieved, level the ground, tread over it lightly, and you are ready to start planting.

surplus water away and prevents the bed becoming saturated.

All the gardens featured in the photographs on pp.92–7 have used raised beds, possibly for reasons other than waterlogging or tree roots. Prime among these factors might be that a raised bed simply looks good, or else that you do not need to bend down so much when planting in them – an advantage that appears ever more appealing the older I get.

What you make the retaining walls of is largely a matter of personal taste, but I think it always looks best if the materials blend with the house construction. For example, the raised bed should be built of brick if the house is of brick; similarly with stone, or rendered or painted concrete, if these are the house facings.

Backfill with garden compost following the same guidelines as previously (*see p.93*), although you might want to add a bit more organic matter, such as well-rotted manure, for general non-treasure planting if the soil is not particularly good.

The problem of tree roots

Simply raising the bed height does not solve the problem of tree roots unless a membrane

Raised beds

Life is rarely that easy. It is more probable that the ground will be saturated or full of tree roots or something similar in the spot that you have identified for shade plants.

In high-rainfall areas, the whole bed should if possible be raised above the surrounding land, even if this is only a matter of 15–23cm (6–9in), because this helps drain

LEFT A muted but restful, low-maintenance planting scheme has been created in these brick raised beds filled primarily with shrubs and easy-care, large perennials such as grassy leaved *Iris sibirica*. The silver-leaved *Artemisia* 'Powis Castle' supplies a successful contrast, yet it is not usually recommended for a shady spot.

RIGHT An action-packed grouping of plants such as this is unfortunately the horticultural equivalent of theatrical stage scenery. It may look good when first put together, but it is unsustainable. The smaller, frailer species will be squeezed out by the more vigorous ones within a season of planting.

of some sort is applied at the outset. Thick polythene, such as that supplied by builders' merchants as waterproof membranes, should be laid within the base of the bed, and drainage holes should be drilled through the base of the walls. Then you can fill the raised bed with your chosen garden compost.

Even a membrane will delay root invasion only for several years, yet it does give your introduced plants plenty of time to establish.

After this honeymoon period, the bed is likely to require more regular watering and feeding than one without a tree-root problem.

A more permanent solution to disruption from tree roots is to concrete the complete area where the raised bed is to stand before building the walls. Care should be taken to limit damage to tree roots during preparation.

Alternatively, you could accept the roots' existence and choose plants to grow in the

LEFT This flower show exhibit would also work satisfactorily as a practical garden. The clean lines and strong colours in this contemporary take on container gardening contrast well with the foliage plants of hostas, heucheras, bamboos, and ferns.

RIGHT A phenomenal roof garden display can be constructed by using solenostemon cultivars, caladium, and the grass *Pennisetum villosum*. Shade is provided by the house walls, containerized conifers, and the ambitiously potted cherry tree.

raised bed that will benefit from them. Bulbs such as cyclamen, erythroniums, and wood anemones are very often quite happy to have tree roots sucking up excess moisture and keeping them dry when they are dormant.

Growing in containers

Pot-grown plants do not suffer from tree root problems at all. The more difficult the site for your shade bed or border, the more likely that containers in some form will play a role in the finished planting scheme. At one extreme, just a single container may be introduced as a focal point, perhaps in conjunction with a raised bed (*see p.92*). Such an idea could be used to extend the interest of a raised bed filled with bulbs. At the other end of the extremity ladder, containers may constitute the whole of the garden on a roof (*right*). A location such as this might well need a shady spot created.

Containers can be used simply, elegantly, and almost architecturally (*above*) in a

minimalistic approach or else they can be set in an intimate, almost fussy way, like a lived-in cluttered room. Although the style you lean towards will depend largely on your personal preferences, it should really take account of the garden ambience and the architectural style of the house or nearby buildings.

Coordinating colours

What is particularly noticeable in the gardens featured in this chapter is that the colour shading of the containers has been carefully matched to the other hard surfacing in every instance. It is a small detail but one that helps to blend everything together. For example, if the location for the containers is on or around a hard-surfaced area near buildings, such as a courtyard or patio, then the finished surface of the buildings and the paving should be taken into account. A modern bricked house or new brick pavers may suggest plain terracotta pots would be the best option, while a modern

house with clean, rendered walls may blend with contemporary containers (*see* p.98) or with simple geometric planters if the anticipated ambience of the finished area is to be for a modern minimalistic simplicity. Older weathered brick pavers and houses may look right with ornate, terracotta containers (*above*), and stone houses may benefit from weathered concrete containers matched so the colour picks up some colour in the stone itself.

Glazed pots in their bewildering range of colours can be used with any house style and age as long as the colour is partially matched. As a general rule, if glazed pots are being used, I prefer to see earth-coloured, matt finished glazes on older properties and those in rural areas, leaving the brighter colours and glossier finishes to more modern and urban environs.

The fun of gardening, though, is taking basic guidelines and then indulging your own preferencies, going where your fancy takes you. So, if you want that scarlet, highly polished, star-shaped pot among your terracotta ones, and it works for you, then go for it, and enjoy.

Potting composts

It is very easy to modify potting compost for containers so that it suits the plants you want to grow. You can add more grit and other drainage materials for bulbs, or introduce more organic matter for plants preferring a richer soil. You can even stand the pot in a shallow container of water if it is to be filled with moisture-loving plants. Always use ericaceous compost for acid-loving plants.

LEFT In late summer, this shady corner still has plenty of colour, with its pink-flowered *Aster trinervius* subsp. *ageratoides* and variegated hostas. Lady's mantle (*Alchemilla mollis*) softens the edges of the hard surfacing and visually links the water trough to the planting beyond.

Foliage or flowers

This flexibility of potting compost also stretches to the choice of using foliage or flowering plants. As a general rule, the more dense the shade the more limited the flowering plant selection will be. There are, however, plants that will grow in shade which have good foliage as well as flowers. For example, many of the epimediums make excellent container plants, as do tricyrtis, hostas, and hardy begonias such as B. *grandis* subsp. *evansiana* and B. *sutherlandii*, among perennials, and notably camellias among shrubs.

If you are tempted to choose plants that are more floriferous, you could position the flowering-plant containers in a brighter location and move them to the shaded bed or border just before they come into flower, provided you have the space in your garden to do this as well as the time. Bear in mind, though, that colours of flowers and non-green foliage look appreciably paler in shade.

BELOW In a half-shady garden, white flowers will glow against the background shadows, especially in evening light. In this London garden, the white–grey theme is enhanced by the use of grey containers and silver-variegated grasses.

LEFT *Helichrysum petiolare* 'Limelight' and white-flowered *Verbena* 'Babylon White' are the dominant plants in these exuberantly planted urns. Very little of this planting will survive the British winters, but this allows for an annual change of "personnel" if so desired.

LEFT In this London garden the choice of plants, although undeniably bold, poses a potential maintenance and sustainability problem. The *Gunnera manicata* with its large leaves is surely going to become too big for this position.

Ease of maintenance

When looking at the garden in London (*left*), I cannot escape the thoughts that it will be very difficult to maintain this space in future years. The golden catalpas would be a good choice for a half-shady garden if they were planted in the ground, but when containerized I wonder how easy it will be to keep them looking lush and healthy without an annual and difficult repot as well as regular fertilizer applications. If some golden foliage were required high up and the plants had to be in containers, I feel a better choice would be the golden-leaved tree *Robinia pseudoacacia* 'Frisia' or possibly climbing golden-leaved hop, which might be allowed to grow over a tripod or some form of trellis.

The gunnera (*left*) is a truly enormous plant with individual leaves capable of growing more than 1.8m (6ft) across. No matter how well designed your site, surely no small garden can incorporate such a monster of a plant. The same effect could easily be created by plants of more manageable proportions. If big leaves are the characteristic required, one of the ornamental rhubarbs, such as *Rheum palmatum* 'Red Herald', with its richly coloured leaves the same shape as the gunnera but only half the size, would be a better choice. Even an ordinary rhubarb plant would work alright. It would also have the bonus that all the stems at least could be eaten after they have inevitably had to be cut off, if the container were positioned so close to the path.

Lushness or simplicity

Another decision has be considered when thinking of garden effects and planting in containers. This is whether to adopt a romantic, lushly planted effect (*above*), with the plants spilling over and largely concealing their containers, or whether to go for a minimalistic simplicity enjoying the lines

LEFT A trelliswork arbour
provides a shady retreat
behind blue-flowered
Ceanothus 'Concha'.
Although the brightly
coloured azalea,
Rhododendron 'Spek's
Orange', draws the eye, it
will be the yellow-flowered
hybrid *R.* 'Narcissiflorum'
and pink-flushed, white
R. occidentale that will fill
the air with scent.

ABOVE Part of the bulb meadow at The Garden House in early spring contains primroses, blue-flowered *Scilla siberica* 'Spring Beauty', and the dwarf daffodils *Narcissus cyclamineus*. The gaps between the plants are home to bulbs that will flower later in the season.

and shapes of the pots as much as the plants themselves (*see* p.104).

Raising the ground level

This is a variation on the raised bed solution for shady beds that have a tree-root problem or are waterlogged. In this, the ground level is altered but there are no supporting walls.

I adopted this approach on an area of ground that would have been classified as difficult at The Garden House. It has heavy shade from a chestnut tree and dry, root-infested soil supporting only a carpet of ivy.

I transformed it (*above and right*) by removing the lower branches of the tree, pulling off the ivy, and raising the beds by 20–30cm (8–12in), so they were above the tree roots and thus easier to plant. The additional height was achieved partly by sinking narrow paths and partly by raiding the compost heap as well as recycling spent compost from the nursery. By landscaping all of this into gently undulating mounds with dips and valleys between, I engineered a whole series of natural-looking raised beds, where bulbs are planted en masse. I have since adopted the

same approach of raising the ground level in my new garden on a much bigger scale, in order to create a wind shelter (*see pp. 88–9*).

Since forming these earth mounds at The Garden House, the chestnut tree roots have grown up into the topsoil. Yet this has made no difference because the bulbs are now established and are nourished by an annual topdressing of a leafmould-based mulch. Into this, the bulbs can self-seed, living out their lives in the top few centimetres/inches of soil. Meanwhile, the tree roots beneath prevent the ground becoming too wet.

Individually, bulbs may be fleeting in flower but collectively they can bring a long period of interest to a site. This part of the garden starts to flower in mid-winter, with the snowdrops, continues through to mid-spring with the usual gang of spring-flowering bulbs such as daffodils, crocus, and wood anemones, as well as perennials such as primroses and hellebores. Flowering then starts again in late summer and early autumn with the appearance of cyclamen, colchicums, and autumn crocus. Six months of colour from bulbs alone – who says they are dull?

COMBINING SHADE-LOVERS

One of the most commonly asked questions regarding shade is what sort of plants can be grown there, and in what styles of gardening?

LEFT Spring-flowering bulbs appear on a large scale in Beth Chatto's garden, where yellow and orange crown Imperials (*Fritillaria imperialis*) rise majestically above pulmonarias and earlier-flowering bulbs. The rather more demure *F. verticillata* grows on the right.

The simple answer is nearly everything if you include the whole range of conditions in different woodland types that are permissible in this broadest context. The topic therefore needs to be broken down into smaller, more specific parts, with each discussed in turn.

At one end of the spectrum of growing conditions is the light shade cast by widely spaced trees in open woodland. The lucky owners of gardens with these conditions probably do not need a book on shade, as they have just about the perfect location for growing a very wide range of plants, even ardent sun-lovers in the most open sections. However, as you move closer to the trees in these gardens, the number of hours of shading will increase. Also, the range of plants itself will alter the nearer you get to the trunks.

Light shade
This slightly shaded area of Bath Chatto's garden (left) would be associated with ground just outside the spread of tall trees. It could also be under the canopy if the trees in question cast only light shade, as with this birch, or else if the trees are heavy shaders and very tall, such as mature pines or Douglas firs, with the lower branches removed.

Such light shade provides optimum conditions for woodland plants. If the site is not a windy, you will be able to grow anything that books, catalogues, and nurserymen say prefer woodland conditions, within the limitations of the acidity of your soil.

Whatever your soil and providing the area is not a major wind funnel, you should consider the idea of selectively removing the lower branches on existing trees and shrubs (*see* p.87), to open up previously unused soil under them, as this really is a woodland gardener's prime real estate.

If the soil conditions are damp, or at minimum cool – the sort of place where ferns regularly appear – then you can probably grow

RIGHT These species of grass mostly prefer full sun, while the bamboo, catching the light in the background, will happily grow in light shade. If its smaller canes are all cut to ground level, leaving just the biggest ones intact, then the effect of the silhouetted clump can be very dramatic.

ABOVE Candelabra primulas are wonderful plants for creating pools of bright colour in cool, preferably damp, half-shady positions. Here *Primula bulleyana* hybrids thrive alongside arum lily (*Zantedeschia aethiopica*) at Merrie Cottage in Hampshire.

candelabra primulas (*above*). In a small area, they would go well with some of the orchids, notably dactylorhizas, the low-growing astilbes, ferns, and small hostas. On a bigger scale, candelabra primulas would look equally good with taller astilbes, hostas, ferns, rodgersias, and arum lilies. These are the usual suspects recommended for bog-gardening, and although they do prefer it damp they do not absolutely demand it. However, most of them will not flower as well if the shade becomes too dense. In a high-rainfall area, I grow all of these plants in full sun, where they flower prolifically. Flowering is likely to be reduced if they are planted in a bed receiving more than three or four hours of shading a day.

Light shade and drier soils

Very free-draining soils combined with shade pose the same sort of questions that tree roots do, resulting in both cases in very dry soil conditions, either because the water drains immediatedly away or because it is soaked up by the roots. If the shading is only light, then grasses can be included in the planting scheme, even though most grasses prefer full sun. With the exception of the bamboos, shade-tolerant grasses (*see* "Plant Directory", *pp*. 169–71) tend to be less than 60cm (2ft) in height.

The most natural and best use of bronze-leaved *Carex comans* I have ever seen was under trees, so I borrowed this idea in my own garden. There, under white-flowering *Hoheria* 'Glory of Amlwch', I undercarpeted the carex with prostrate, blue-flowered *Pratia pedunculata*. It turns out that all of these three plants are native to New Zealand.

Woodland plants are often quite restrained, and the accepted good taste of shade gardens is

RIGHT This "cool" arrangement will not need much maintenance, other than cutting the blue catmint and yellow lady's mantle down after flowering. The latter job is very important unless you want seedlings of this self-sowing perennial appearing everywhere.

LEFT Designer Sharon Osmund has created a very subtle arrangement in the corner of this garden. It is a grouping that will work well even in quite dense shade, but it will require significant modification and thinning as it matures, to maintain its overall balance.

for subtle hues, as perhaps befits the dappled light. However, in light shade there is no reason why you cannot opt for a rather more flamboyant colour range. On lighter, free-draining soils you could enjoy the riot of spring colour afforded by tulips (*see p.135*) or summer bedding. Alternatively, you could fill the space with fuchsias or bedded-out lilies. These would not be my personal choice, but how boring it would be if everyone had the same preferences in gardening.

An adaptable planting design

From Sharon Osmund's garden (*left*), you can glean a lot of information (much of which has already been touched on in earlier chapters), which could be adapted to a "problem" shade area, however dense the shading.

Her choice of plants are mainly foliage ones and primarily green coloured, which means a balanced design such as this could be achieved in any shady area. These plants are mostly growing in the ground, but the same effect could be achieved with containers and raised beds (*see "Planting in Shade", pp.92–109*).

The fencing provides an interesting and appropriate vertical element, and the hard landscaping – from the mulch to the various uses of statuary and stones – provide focal and talking points.

This particular scheme has many plants, probably to create an instant effect. However, I think it would look just as good if there were half the number of plants, to open up vistas to the statuary, as well as a larger mulched area.

Full shade

These are areas where very little direct sunlight falls. It is not the same as saying no light

reaches the ground, because on sunny days I would hope that narrow spears of sunlight will fleetingly spotlight plants in a constantly changing light show. Like taking pictures of wildlife, the onlooker needs to be quick to catch these subtle light effects in this magical world of dancing shadows.

Foliage plants come into their own in this location, providing the main staple of gardens in full shade. Many plants will flower well in deepish shade, but they tend not to be of the massively showy variety and are none the worse for that.

Shade and its effect on colour

You should be aware that variegation is not constantly reliable in shady conditions. Some variegated plants hold their colour well, while other varieties that are superficially similar do not do so. There are no hard and fast rules regarding which coloured-foliage types will retain their colour in full shade, and you just need to experiment.

If there were any generalization to be made, it would be that most coloured-foliaged plants (that is, other than plain green) will tend to be paler than identical plants growing in full sun, and the shadier the conditions the more likely the leaves are to revert to green – purple-foliaged plants being especially prone to do this.

This paling of colour applies just as much to some flower colours. Yellow, white, and blue are usually unaffected in their intensity by shading, but many – though not all – reds and pinks are noticeably paler in shady conditions. If a plant is not performing well or up to expectations in one set of conditions, for example full shade, it may be worth moving it to somewhere with more light. This applies just as much in reverse.

Partial shade-loving Himalayan blue poppies (various *Meconopsis* species) always

RIGHT Many Japanese woodland plants possess an indefinable quality. For example, this Japanese painted fern (*Athyrium niponicum* var. *pictum*) will hold its subtle coloration best in almost full shade. Here its form and colour are perfectly offset by the glossy leaves of asarum.

LEFT The trees behind Christopher Bradley-Hole's inspired Chelsea exhibit are rather misleading, suggesting this display is for a shady garden whereas these plants would certainly demand nearly full sun. The planting principle though, using different plants, is still valid for a shady garden if a modern approach is wanted.

ABOVE The variegated grass *Hakonechloa macra* 'Aureola' is a magnificent choice for shady gardens, as it looks good all through the season. In early autumn, it can make a fine partnership with some of the toad lilies, in this case *Tricyrtis* 'Tojen', which "burn" in sun.

excite interest bordering on disbelief for people who have not seen them before. In healthy, happy plants, the blue of their flowers is an almost unreal pure colour with no trace of pink. The colour of their blooms can be influenced by weather conditions in the month before they flower, and should it be too dry and hot for their liking the flower colour will markedly shade towards purple. The same plants the following year if the season is cooler can once again revert back to immaculate blue.

Ferns

If there was one type of plant more than any other that thoroughly relishes woodland conditions it would have to be ferns. They are perfectly adapted to the darkest shade, and their shapes and textures make them a must-have for the shade gardener.

As you will see from the photographs in this chapter, ferns can be combined with strong foliage plants, with flowering plants, with water, statuary, paving, and – very simply

and effectively – with moss. They make excellent container plants, and in fact I can think of no planting scheme that would not benefit from a suitably chosen fern.

Nowadays, ferns can even provide strong vertical elements if you are fortunate enough to be able to afford large specimens of the tree ferns. These magnificent plants really do not like windy conditions, however. Given the right location, a group of tall tree ferns planted 2–3m (6½–10ft) apart would create vertical structure and wonderful shade for a bed or border beneath, producing in effect a living pergola. It is one idea that I shall certainly pursue in my own garden when I can conjure a bit of freedom from excessive wind.

Oriental simplicity

Shade gardening is one area where you could borrow ideas from ancient gardening practices in the Orient. Over the centuries, the Japanese have perfected the use of plants and hard landscaping in shady areas and have taken the art to great heights of stylized beauty.

Try and recreate these by all means if this suits your space, but I feel more excited by how the general oriental principles can be modified to produce hybrid fusions that are neither eastern or western (such as in the garden on p.54). This approach, particularly, has possibilities where lush planting may not be practicable, as in dense shade or with those dreaded tree roots. In such areas, modified versions of Japanese shade gardens may just provide some lateral-thinking inspiration. Borrow a book on Japanese gardening from the library and go through it, but not necessarily to copy ideas. Consciously consider how you might change or modify their designs to suit your own situation.

LEFT Magnificently exotic effects can be produced in shade using bold foliage plants such as in this masterly creation, which invokes a prehistoric atmosphere, when dinosaurs roamed the world. With care, a similarly tropical effect can be achieved in temperate climates. To do well, such a planting scheme would need to be in a very sheltered site.

BELOW The fern *Woodwardia fimbriata* here contributes to an oriental "feel" because of the way it has been utilized in conjunction with the rocks and the water feature. This mood is further strengthened by the planting of the Japanese katsura tree (*Cercidiphyllum japonicum*) on the left of the fern.

Waterside planting

These two gardens (*above* and *right*) demonstrate another manifestation of how this east/west fusion might work and how it might lead on to other exciting planting possibilities.

Imagine the Japanese garden in Portland (*right*) with the shrubs alongside the stream removed but everything else left intact. Then replace the shrubs with astilbes, such as in the garden illustrated above, and perhaps add in some low-growing hostas or shade-tolerant grasses as well. In this very simple way you have changed a Japanese garden into a western one with a vague eastern "feel".

Hostas, hostas everywhere

The superabundance of hostas in shady gardens is mainly because they are easy to cultivate – subject, of course, to the slugs – and their undoubted handsomeness. But to my eye, and perhaps here is the rub, hostas are only handsome and not beautiful. I do not know whether my viewpoint is connected with their ubiquitousness.

In the same way, I find it difficult to wax lyrical about laburnums, forsythias, and the Japanese cherries *Prunus* 'Kanzan' and P. 'Amanogawa', as they have almost become "invisible" so frequently do they occur.

RIGHT The combined planting of lady fern (*Athyrium filix-femina*) and moss serves to link all the other elements in this Japanese garden in Portland, Oregon.

RIGHT In this London garden, hostas are the star players. They are excellent as container plants in shade gardens, looking good all season, and are content to remain in the same pot for years.

BELOW By contrast, hostas are just part of the view in this woodland garden. The taller, non-variegated hosta particularly looks very natural planted alongside the fence, where it makes a bold counterpoint to the hovering orange flowers of the aquilegias.

As with all my generalizations, this one is as watertight as a colander, because the tall vase-shaped hostas (*below*) look perfect as accent plants in a setting like this. Varieties such as H. 'Krossa Regal' and H. 'Snowden' have an elegant bearing, which makes them perfect as specimens standing proud of lower-growing plants in shady spots. To compound further the illogical nature of my prejudice, hostas with tall thin flowering stems, such as H. 'Royal Standard', with its scented white flowers and plain green leaves, are definitely beautiful.

Restraint is probably the key to planting with hostas, and in most of the gardens here they are being used in a limited and effective way. Like ferns, hostas can look good with just

about anything, and there are varieties to suit planting combinations on any level, from small woodland treasures to perennial plantings on the boldest scale. However, unlike ferns, their bold coloration and often large leaves unfailingly draw the eye. This can prove to be both their strength and their weakness.

Used wisely, hostas are natural focal points to any planting, but overdone and with many different varieties planted in the same bed, especially singletons, the eye darts around from one to the next and cannot settle. The planting becomes anything but restful. Plant this way by all means if you want a collection of hostas, but be cautious following this route if aesthetics are important to you.

I would suggest planting hostas in groups of at least three. When using variegated varieties, try to choose a colour range that will link with neighbouring plants. For example, in this coordinated colour scheme, white-variegated hostas have been planted beneath white-flowered dicentra (*below*). Similarly, blue-leaved hostas look good surrounded by perennials with a blue-green tinge, and ditto golden-variegated varieties with yellow-green foliage and ferns (*right*). This cosy arrangement can

form the core of a planting, perhaps being broken up with the odd plant that deliberately bucks the trend to draw the eye while at the same time keeping the design restful.

Doubling up with bulbs

With some of the larger and later-emerging hostas, such as *H. sieboldiana*, it is possible to grow early-flowering bulbs actually in the hosta's crown, therefore doubling the value from the same ground space. This is the same principle – albeit on a micro scale – as natural growth patterns in woods themselves, with spring-flowering plants taking advantage of extra light through the bare branches before being shaded in summer by the trees' canopy. One of the reasons this works with hostas is because their root system is composed of relatively large fleshy roots, leaving small pockets of earth between them. Although large, hosta leaves channel some of the rain that falls on them back to the centre of the plant, resulting in other plants sheltering underneath not becoming too dry.

This same technique works even better with the bold-leaved rodgersias, which similarly are late leafing out in spring. However, I would not suggest you try to grow bulbs in the crowns of rodgersias if

LEFT The white bleeding heart *Dicentra spectabilis* 'Alba' lends height and form to a handsome small grouping in the corner of a shady bed. The white theme is picked up by the pale centre to the bright green leaves of attractive *Hosta undulata* var. *univittata*.

RIGHT Success in combining plants is largely a matter of personal taste. My own feeling is that ferny leaves work best with the big rounded leaves of hostas when there are a lot of them, as is the case with the dicentra and fern in this planting scheme.

you are cultivating them in permanently damp conditions for which they are frequently recommended, as the bulbs are likely to rot. Doubling up works with other late-emerging perennials, such as tall-growing filipendulas and *Thalictrum delavayi*, as well.

I have also successfully grown snowdrops and wood anemones in this way, and I imagine it would be possible with other early woodland bulbs, such as winter aconites, as well. It is more doubtful whether it would work satisfactorily with bulbs such as daffodils and crocus which enjoy a summer baking.

Other bold-leaved accent plants

It is important to include contrasting types of foliage in your designs for shade planting. I prefer a very limited use of variegated plants in a woodland setting, as I feel the textures, shapes, and many shades of plain green are more sympathetic to that situation. Restricting your palette primarily to green, though, does

necessitate the use of bold-foliaged plants. Fortunately, hostas are not the only plants that have this characteristic.

In the illustrated garden (left), the boldness and drama are provided by the phlomis, its yellow flowers standing out from the dark background almost as if spotlighted. This same effect can be deliberately engineered by planting background shrubs with purple foliage such as purple corylus or Japanese maples. In this garden, *Cotinus coggygria* 'Royal Purple' was an inspired choice, taking not only the purple and green colours through the composition but also a similar leaf shape. The only problem for a shady garden is that this sort of planting requires a reasonably well-lit site, and the greater the shade the more the purple hues would fade into insignificance.

Rodgersias, too, are superb foliage plants. Their large, well-textured leaves are as bold as any hostas, but their usual pinnate form means they will combine readily with plants bearing smaller or more delicate leaves such as ferns. With gently wandering roots, their habit is informal so in naturalistic plantings they are easy to incorporate into woodland schemes. Their flowers are like the tall, rigid plumes of an astilbe, and they age to an often beetroot-red colour, which lasts for months. However, rodgersias will not flower if planted in too much shade.

They are able to cope with permanently damp soil but do not demand it. In several species and varieties, their young emerging leaves are strikingly copper, bronzed, or brown in colour. Particularly good in this respect are *R. pinnata* 'Superba', *R. aesculifolia*, *R.* 'Irish Bronze', and *R. podophylla* 'Rotlaub', but there are many more, and most of them display this trait to a greater or lesser extent.

Dense shade

This type of shade is not really appropriate territory for growing bulbs. Most of those suitable are native to deciduous woodlands or among widely spaced conifers, where by one means or another the light reaching them in their periods of growth is at worst only gently filtered. For this reason, most bulbs tend to flower in spring, when they can produce spectacular floral displays.

Wood anemones are classic woodland "bulbous" plants, even though the botanists will be quick to point out they are perennials with rhizomes. Like snowdrops, wood anemones in the wild are capable of producing enormous drifts of flowers in suitable woods or of toughing it out in the hedgerows. This adaptive quality means that both wood anemones and snowdrops are well suited

ABOVE Woodland bulbs that flower after the main spring rush are often taller in growth, and *Camassia leichtlinii* subsp. *leichtlinii* is no exception. Its architectural flower spikes last for several weeks, and they look especially good when appearing between shrubs or taller perennials, such as this *Lysimachia ciliata* 'Firecracker'.

to mixed plantings in the shady garden. They happily share space with anyone who will have them and so are perfect for blending and imparting unity to a bed or even whole sections of garden, as with the tulips of Keukenhof in The Netherlands (*right*).

Tulip displays are definitely for areas with no more than light shade, as these large-flowered hybrids were originally bred from species native to the Mediterranean area, where they mostly grow in full sun. Two tulip species tolerate woodland conditions and are perennial. These are *T. sylvestris*, which has yellow flowers but tends not to be very free-flowering, and *T. sprengeri*, which bears red flowers in late spring.

No bulbs that are reliably perennial can compete with such eye-popping colour as the hybrid tulips, and for many gardeners that is probably no bad thing. They may be spectacular but their colour is hardly restful, and the more restrained effects of those bulbous plants which come up year on year are just as welcome.

Woodland floral calendar

Magnificent displays of spring bulbs can be enjoyed in light woodland or semi-shady

BELOW In spring, massed
ranks of tulips with some
crown imperials (top left)
thrown in for contrast
provide eye-catching
blocks of colour in
Keukenhof gardens in
The Netherlands. Such
a design may not be to
everyone's taste, but it
is undeniably colourful.

gardens in the whole colour spectrum range except for orange and red.

I look forward every year to the woodland bulb flower show that starts with snowdrops, then blue-purple reticulate irises, pink, carmine, or white *Cyclamen coum*, crocuses of many colours, yellow daffodils, blue chionodoxas and scillas, blue and white wood anemones, yellow-white and pink erythroniums continue into mid-spring. When you realize that several of these genera have

dozens, even hundreds, of named forms you begin to get some idea of the options available.

When combined with shade-loving perennials such as primroses, hellebores, pulmonarias, phlox, trilliums, cardamines, and corydalis, to name but a few of the flowering genera, you really start to open up the planting possibilities. And I have not even mentioned any foliage plants that can be added, such as ferns and hostas. If all of these various elements are allowed to spread and

LEFT Both white-flowered *Lilium martagon* and *Geranium pratense* are capable of naturalizing in light woodland, even among thin grass. They achieve this by self-seeding so there must be gaps among adjacent plants for the seedlings to develop.

NEXT PAGE The benefit of pale-coloured flowers seen against a dark background is very evident in this planting of Asiatic lilies, spotlit by evening sun. Such a setting is enhanced by the lure of a gateway or arch with sunlight beyond.

become an integral part of the bed as well as a convenient perch.

Some gaps left unplanted and mulched with bark for example would achieve the same result in the short term, but would soon fall prey to self-sown seedlings or the running roots of the dicentra.

Later-flowering bulbs

Not altogether surprisingly, the range of woodland bulbous plants that flower after the spring rush is quite limited. In a natural habitat, once the tree canopy has closed over and perennial plants at ground level have reached maximum annual growth, there is little opportunity or space for any would-be opportunistic bulb to flourish. To cope with competing vegetation, any bulbs would need to grow quite tall or occupy the edges of woodland, where the light levels are greater.

Camassia can cope with such conditions. This bulbous plant, which comes into flower in late spring, ranges in height from dark blue-flowered *C. quamash* at 30–45cm (1–1½ft) to white- or blue-flowered *C. leichtlinii* at 1.2m (4ft). Both are good for naturalizing in light woodland, and they die away by mid-summer.

Arisaemas are classic summer-flowering woodland bulbs and are members of the arum

LEFT At the Royal Horticultural Society garden at Wisley, Surrey, woodland bulbs and perennials completely cover the ground during spring. The main contributors are the pink lockets of dicentra and blue-flowered scilla, with assistance from wood anemones and hellebores.

seed, then very varied and rich tapestries of spring-flowering plants can be achieved.

On a practical level, this blending or allowing plants to grow into each other can be problematic to some gardeners. The aim is to achieve a natural-looking tapestry of flowers, but when plants are packed together tightly (left) where exactly do you stand to do any necessary weeding? The answer, as in this case, is to incorporate some flat stones into the design which, when weathered and mossed,

RIGHT Erythroniums, like many plants with downward-facing flowers, are well worth bending down to investigate, because very often the inside of the flowers can be beautifully marked. This as yet unnamed hybrid is no exception.

FAR RIGHT *Trillium grandiflorum* is one of the best wake robins for a gardener as the flowers last for several weeks. However, they often fade to pink as they age. Here *T. grandiflorum* thrives between blue *Corydalis flexuosa* 'Père David' and the yellow bells of *Uvularia grandiflora*.

LEFT Snowdrops and hellebores are a winning combination in late winter. Here, double and semi-double hellebores, bred by a champion breeder of the genus, Robin White, grow in his private garden in Hampshire.

family to which lords-and-ladies (*Arum maculatum*) belongs. They have similar hooded, cloaked "flowers" except they are nearly always in green, brown, or maroon-red.

Roscoeas are exotic-looking plants happy to grow in lightly shaded spots. Their strap-shaped leaves and terminal flower heads appear very orchid-like. Different species flower from spring through to early autumn, with colours ranging from nearly white, through lemon-yellow to royal purple and even terracotta-red. Roscoeas range in height from 30cm (1ft) to 60cm (2ft).

Lilies provide a feast of blooms during summer. Countless years of plant hybridizing has resulted in innumerable lily varieties to suit most height requirements, from 45cm (18in) to 2m (6½ft) high. They basically still

share that need for edge-of-wood light, which translates to partial shade. Lilies can be scented and subtle or as colourful as Keukenhof tulips, but no garden with half-shady conditions should be without some at least.

Indulge a bulb passion

Throughout this book, I have tried to tread a tightrope between spinning a positive attitude towards what are often considered problem areas and being very enthusiastic for the fabulous plants that can be grown in good woodland conditions. I did not want to alienate those struggling with the basics of this way of gardening by describing at length the glories of what may have seemed unattainable. It would be like waxing lyrical on the beauties of the latest swimwear fashions for wraith like

ABOVE *Cyclamen coum* creates a tapestry of pink which for its rich colouring can rarely be beaten for late winter/early spring effect. As a result of considerable dedication by relatively few breeders and growers, *C. coum* is now available with leaves that range from glossy green to all-silver, and everything in between.

models when you are 13kg (28lb) overweight and contemplating going on a diet. I do not, however, want to finish without extolling the excitement woodland plants can generate.

In my garden in the sky, there will be orchards of lichen-encrusted fruit trees with twisted and gnarled trunks like those in this orchard (*right*). The shadows of these trunks will dance across sheets of crocus and patches of snowdrops together with isolated clumps of hellebores and swathes of cyclamen. Later,

wood anemones and dwarf daffodils will paint this orchard yellow, white, and blue, and erythroniums will be everywhere. This may be a dream, but it is not impossible in the actual world you live in.

If land prices are as steep in heaven as they are down here, maybe I will have to settle for a small rectangular plot behind the house. If this were the case, so much do I love this type of garden that I would have to create shade if none existed. I could cover the whole area with a modified pergola with widely spaced timbers on the top and grow a wisteria or two to cover over this framework partially and to provide an ever-changing patchwork of sunlight and shadows on the ground beneath, as the sun arches across the sky.

Underneath in raised beds, so as better to appreciate their beauty, I will grow all the candidates from my orchard only in smaller numbers, as well as orchids, small ferns, corydalis, shortias, wake robins, and as many other of these wonderful woodland plants as I could squeeze in. I hope horticulture is still an option if and when it is my turn to approach those famous gates.

Being positive

When I set out to write this book, my aim and hope was to instil a positive attitude towards your shady corners, wherever you garden. If trees are responsible for the shading, I hope you might now go and take a closer look at any woods near you to see if there are any lessons you might learn.

Back in your own garden, you may want to consider taking off a few lower branches on a tree (*see pp.87–8*), and I would always explore this option before contemplating removing the tree altogether. It is amazing how much

BELOW Magical moments, such as finding these beautiful *Crocus tommasinianus* flowering in late winter beneath old fruit trees, have to be seized. As with all crocuses, the flowers will not open properly unless the sun shines, so in occasional gloomy years they hardly open at all.

LEFT The Winterthur Garden in Delaware is among the very best shade gardens in the USA, and it is easy to see why when there are wildflowers as good as these buttercups and wild blue phlox. This part of the garden shows natural woodland gardening at its peak.

ABOVE This is artistic woodland gardening as practised at a top level by Beth Chatto in her garden in Essex. She personally has done as much as anyone in the UK to promote this style of gardening, in which she uses mostly perennials and woodland bulbs.

extra light you will let in if branches are removed up to half the overall height of the tree. A good arborist should be able to advise on maintaining the aesthetic balance of the tree, which may require only crown thinning to allow more light to reach the ground.

Once you have maximized the light levels in the shady area, then the fun can begin as you draw up your planting designs and are inspired to enjoy these magical shady retreats. You may even become hooked on the merits of woodland plants.

PLANT DIRECTORY

It could take a whole book to produce a comprehensive list of plants suitable for shade. I have therefore concentrated here on tried-and-tested genera, relying on my personal experiences with them. As a guide to hardiness I have used the zone system devised by the United States Department of Agriculture (USDA).

Trees and shrubs

Because the primary role of tall, forest trees is to create shelter and shade, in this section I have described only small trees and shrubs that are able to grow in shady conditions. These naturally provide shade of their own, as does any plant if you keep scaling down in size.

Dense shade above and strong light to the side will cause nearly all trees and shrubs to grow towards the light, and thus lopsidedly. In my last garden, trees planted even 20m (60ft) away on the south side of 30m (100ft) high lime trees still slanted towards the south. The higher the canopy is raised on shading trees, by removing lower branches, the less such leaning will occur.

ACER MAPLE

In a genus of more than 100 species it is only the shrubby or small tree types which are relevant for growing in shade. Any of the smaller-growing species tolerate light shade, and many even succeed in almost full shade provided there is enough space above them to develop into as well as relatively constant light levels. Japanese maples are especially good, although coloured-leaved varieties will be less intense and become increasingly green the denser the shade. Their growth habit will also be thinner and rather more elongated, yet they are none the worse for that, with those varieties cultivated for their autumn colour still performing well, even if a little bit less intensely than in more open positions.

Nearly a quarter of all acer species grow in Japan, but what gardeners

Acer palmatum

generally regard as Japanese maples are varieties of just A. *japonicum* and more importantly A. *palmatum*. Both species and their varieties are winter hardy above ground to −18°C (0°F) but suffer root damage if subjected to temperatures below −10°C (14°F), so hardy in Zone 6. There are several hundred varieties of these two species, and given space I would grow them all. The vast majority of those sold are varieties of A. *palmatum*, and these range in size from small trees, maturing eventually to 10m (30ft) high, to weeping shrubs, which are rarely larger than 2m (6½ft). Two of the most popular types are the taller-growing, purple-leaved varieties, such as A.p 'Bloodgood', and the weeping shrubby ones with feathery leaves often referred to as the "dissectum" maples.

A.p 'Bloodgood' has an upright, vase-shaped growth reaching about 3 x 2.4m (10 x 8ft), while the dissectums make dome-shaped bushes 1m (3ft) high and across. The dissectums are perfect for growing in containers, as open-ground specimens, and alongside water or hard landscaping. Being slow growing, they are very suitable for small gardens. The green-leaved variety is A.p.var. *dissectum* Dissectum Viride Group, and among the many purple-leaved ones A.p.var. *dissectum* 'Garnet' and the taller more open A.p.var. *dissectum* 'Inaba-shidare' are among the most reliable, both turning scarlet in autumn.

AMELANCHIER SNOWY MESPILUS

These small trees or multi-trunked shrubs are of similar size and habit to the Japanese maples, reaching about 4 x 4m (12½ x 12½ft), and would look very good growing with them in open woodland. Several of the amelanchiers have a very long period of beauty, with purple young leaves accompanied in spring by white or pink-flushed flowers. Autumn colour can be a bonfire of red, orange, and yellow.

In rural areas birds are very prone to strip their flower buds so these trees are more frequently seen in residential areas, especially on acidic soils. They are often

Amelanchier canadensis

planted on the boundaries of these gardens, where they are trimmed into hedges. Amelanchiers respond very well to this treatment. However, their full beauty is not fully realized unless they are grown as individual trees or in a group. If the lower branches are then removed, you would create a very desirable planting location beneath for shade-loving plants.

The best species for general planting are A. *laevis* and A. *lamarckii*, both with attractively coloured young foliage enhancing the flowers as well as good autumn colour. They prefer acidic soils and are winter hardy in zone 4. A. *canadensis* is even hardier (Zone 3) and has a suckering shrubby habit to 3m (10ft) with upright stems. All do well in damp sites.

Camellia x *williamsii* 'E.T.R. Carlyon'

CAMELLIA

As long as your soil is neutral or acidic, camellias are undoubtedly the best evergreen shrubs that can be grown in shade. Even if they never flowered I would still grow them just for their glossy dark green leaves, which provide the perfect foil to set off plants in front. Camellias do not demand shade and in fact they generally flower better in a sunnier site. When established, they are surprisingly wind-tolerant. Typically camellias make upright shrubs eventually growing into trees up to 10m (30ft) high, yet they are also extremely amenable to being pruned. They even tolerate being cut with a hedge-trimmer if necessary, and so can be kept to virtually any size. Pruning should be done soon after the shrubs have flowered.

There are, of course, many, many varieties of camellia to choose from, in fact literally thousands, but they all bear glossy evergreen foliage. Typically, common camellia (*C. japonica*) (Zone 7) produces rounded leaves and flowers of bewildering variation of form and colour. Although very beautiful when fresh, the flowers of some varieties of this species do not look particularly good as they fade, especially if their petals do not drop to the ground.

C. japonica is one of the parents of a group of hybrids known as *C.* x *williamsii* (Zone 7), among which white-flowered *C.* x *w.* 'E.T.R. Carlyon' is fairly typical. Generally, these offspring do drop their older flowers, and thus they are better for overall garden effect.

Recommending varieties of camellia is very challenging because they are nearly all good and so choice depends to a considerable extent on personal preferencies. However, were I restricted to just one camellia it would have to be the white-flowered *C.* 'Cornish Snow' (Zone 7). This covers itself from top to bottom with small, white, single flowers produced in such numbers that, even if frosted, there will be more buds waiting to take their turn.

CORYLOPSIS

These are shrubs for light shade and thus ideal for locations at the edge of woods or under tall trees. The main period of beauty for corylopsis is in early spring, when their leafless branches are hung with drooping racemes of pale yellow, scented flowers, transforming the bushes into clouds of soft yellow. In autumn, the rather hazel-like leaves turn a clear yellow, typically having been an unassuming green during summer.

The habit of many corylopsis species is upright and funnel-shaped or open and spreading, growing to about 4m (12½ft) in height. One exception is densely branched *C. pauciflora* (Zone 6), which is a class act and should be in every shady garden. It may eventually reach 1.5m (5ft) in height and width after many years, but more often it attains nearer to half that size. After covering itself in flowers, the small leaves emerge purple flushed before changing to green and then a rich yellow in autumn – it is one of the stars of that season for me.

Corylopsis spicata

to cultivate in all soils, although the evergreens cope better with dense shade.

The two main evergreen species likely to be encountered are *E. fortunei* (Zone 6) and *E. japonicus* (Zone 6) in their various guises. *E. fortunei* is altogether smaller and easier to find. It has several very good variegated varieties including *E.f.* 'Silver Queen' (Zone 6) and the golden *E.f.* 'Emerald 'n Gold' (Zone 6). Both grow 30–60cm (1–2ft) high and have a mildly trailing habit. They tolerate pruning to whatever size you want. Both varieties are very good at providing low pools of colour throughout the year and, being very compact, of giving some wind protection to frailer neighbours.

Because *E. japonicus* is larger than *E. fortunei*, it is less popular among gardeners where space is always a constraint. However, *E. japonicus*

Even in winter its intricate branch and twig structure is handsome. Unfortunately *C. pauciflora* needs acid soil, because it is the only member of the genus that is not lime-tolerant. No corylopsis appreciates being planted in thin soils.

At Winterthur in Delaware, the taller-growing species of corylopsis have been planted en masse under tall trees. They bloom at the same time as blue-flowered *Rhododendron augustinii* (Zone 7) – a truly

magical sight. *C. spicata* (Zone 7), from Japan, has a more spreading habit growing perhaps 2 x 3m (6½ x 10ft), but its flowers are typical of the genus.

EUONYMUS

This genus has two distinct types: the evergreen species and the deciduous ones (which include the spindle berries). Both are suitable for planting in shade and are easy

Euonymus fortunei 'Silver Queen'

Hedera helix 'Tricolor'

'Président Gauthier' (Zone 6), with its variegated leaves, is well worth searching for. I grew this variety for many years and it remained a well-behaved shrub of about 2m (6½ft) high, not changing much from one year to the next. Then one day it just decided to start climbing up the nearby wall and within two years it had reached 8m (25ft). It was as if it had experienced a mid-life crisis and decided it was now or never for a change in shape.

The deciduous spindles are large shrubs, really only beautiful in autumn, so are good for large woodland gardens.

HEDERA IVY

Ivies are neither trees or shrubs (except in their occasional arborescent forms), being climbers happy on a horizontal or vertical plane. They are particularly valuable for shady areas of the garden where little else would grow. Because they tolerate dry,

Hydrangea serrata 'Shishiva'

dense shade, I can see why ivies are recommended for these places but I cannot bring myself to like them. Perhaps I spent too long as a child exploring ivy-covered woods with their ominous, brooding atmosphere, so now that distinctive smell conjures up negative associations. Although ivies do the job of covering the ground well, there are more exciting plant options available for flat areas.

Using ivies to climb vertically is a different matter. They can be really good growing against walls, fences, over trellises, or up tree trunks, where they can provide dark, almost black backgrounds (in the case of the green varieties) or pools of colour shining from dark corners (when some of the variegated forms are chosen). I remember a wall in the National Trust garden at Hidcote, Gloucestershire, covered in the golden leaves of *H. helix* 'Buttercup' (Zone 5). It appeared for all the world as if bathed in sunshine – even on a dull day.

I have also successfully grown variegated ivies such as *H.h.* 'Tricolor' (Zone 5) against a wall where deciduous flowering shrubs, such as chaenomeles, have been trained in the same place. The result is a doubling of interest, with the ivy looking good during the winter months. Both varieties mentioned are capable of climbing 5m (15ft) or more but can readily be pruned to remain much smaller.

HYDRANGEA

These deciduous and evergreen shrubs and climbers grow in a wide range of conditions where the soil is not too dry but they seem to look best in woodland gardens. The hydrangeas most often encountered are varieties of deciduous *H. macrophylla*: this has two flowering forms – the mopheads and the lacecaps.

There are so many superficially similar mopheads that, if possible, it is best to buy them when in flower. One that has stood the test of time is *H.m.* 'Générale Vicomtesse de Vibraye' (Zone 7), which grows up to 2m (6½ft) high and wide. On acid soils, its flowers are a very good, almost turquoise-blue; they are vivid pink on limey soils. Flower colour is very sensitive to alkalinity and even slow-release fertilizers added in very small amounts by the nurseryman can turn hydrangeas pink.

In lacecap hydrangeas, the fertile central florets in the flower head are surrounded by infertile ray florets. These two sections of the head are often of different colours and lend an almost two-tone effect to this type of hydrangea, as in *H. serrata* 'Shishiva' (Zone 7).

Other species of hydrangea mostly have lacecap flower heads, and nearly all of them prefer some light shading, especially the bigger-leaved types which can get burnt by the sun. In late summer *H. paniculata* (Zone 4) bears pyramidal heads of white flowers that age red. It makes a shrub 3m (10ft) high and wide unless it has been pruned. *H. paniculata* can be cut back virtually to the ground each year, as you might treat a winter-stemmed dogwood. There are plenty more hydrangea species should you get hooked

KALMIA MOUNTAIN LAUREL, CALICO BUSH

Mountain laurel (*K. latifolia*) (Zone 4) is native to the eastern states of the USA, where winter temperatures can be very cold, particularly in the northern half of its

Kalmia latifolia

Rhododendron 'Kirin'

range, so it is very hardy. It does, however, need acid soil that is free-draining. It generally grows to 2 x 1.5m (6½ x 5ft) and is an understorey shrub of woods in the wild, where I have seen it growing in quite dense shade. However in the UK, where summers tend not to be so hot as in its native eastern USA, mountain laurel needs more sun to flower freely and herein lies the rub. You can either plant it in full sun to flower freely where the leaves can start to turn yellow, or you can grow it in shade and risk reduced flowering.

You may wonder why bother to grow it at all, until you see mountain laurel in full flower in early summer, when there are so few competitors. At The Garden House, which is on a north slope with 1,500mm (60in) of rain yearly, I planted dozens of them in full sun on banks, and they grew and flowered beautifully, becoming a highlight of that month's flowering.

Nearly all the mountain laurels are similar in habit and leaf, varying only in their flower and bud colour. The species itself is good but being almost certainly seed-raised will vary, so look out for consistent, vegetatively propagated named forms such as *K.l.* 'Ostbo Red' (with its vivid sealing-wax red buds and pink flowers) and *K.l.* 'Freckles' (with its pale pink flowers and each petal spotted with purple). When mature, these varieties have a similar size, habit, and hardiness as the species.

Other species, notably *K. angustifolia* (Zone 1), grow in damp soils but they are smaller, forming spreading thickets about 1m (3ft) high. They are also not as showy as mountain laurel.

PIERIS

Although these evergreen shrubs need lime-free soil, they would still make my desert-island "top 10" list of shrubs. For sheer year-round value, some of the pieris take some beating. They are principally grown for the colour of their young leaves, which for a month or so in spring are as bright red as any flowers, rather like the houseplant poinsettia. Gradually these leaves turn through orange, then yellow and on to plain green.

In late summer at the tips of the shoots, the sprays of flower buds are set for the following year, and in some cases these are noticeably red-tinged and are quite a feature all through the winter months. *P. formosa* var. *forrestii* 'Jermyns' (Zone 7) and *P. japonica* 'Dorothy Wyckoff' (Zone 7) are particularly good in this respect. Both grow to about 2 x 1.5m (6½ x 5ft), but the former has a more open habit. *P. formosa* var *forrestii* (Zone 7) is also of similar size but with a more upright growth habit, less colourful flower buds, and brilliantly coloured young leaves. Towards the end of winter, the buds open into lily of the valley-like sprays of generally white flowers, which hum to the wings of early bees. Thereafter, the whole cycle begins again.

Many pieris also have beautiful cinnamon-coloured trunks. Two of the best pieris are hybrids and very similar to each other. They are *P.* 'Firecrest' (Zone 6) and *P.* 'Forest Flame' (Zone 6), both making columnar shrubs eventually 3 x 1.5m (10 x 5ft). There are also a few attractive variegated varieties of pieris.

RHODODENDRON

This truly is an enormous group of plants which can be the very bedrock of a woodland garden as virtually all of them will be at home in light shade. The genus includes the hybrid rhododendrons as well as deciduous azaleas, evergreen azaleas, and the amazingly varied rhododendron species, which can range from a few centimetres to tree height. Rhododendrons have flowers to match, some being as small as your thumbnail, while others produce flower trusses as big as a basketball.

There are hybrid rhododendrons in all the colours of the rainbow and in all sizes, so choose to taste, and enjoy. Species rhododendrons are more of an acquired

taste but are remarkably varied and beautiful, although generally not quite so straightforward and easy to grow as the hybrids. I love many of them – too many to mention in fact.

Some species are deciduous and sometimes get lumped under deciduous azaleas. They are in fact some of the original parents of the zillions of hybrid deciduous azaleas now available. They are all beautiful with some colours rather more in your face than others, but I like those that have a scent. Many flower in late spring, and their fragrance is locked in my memory with that of bluebells, which flower at the same time and happen to look fantastic growing with rhododendron.

Evergreen azaleas are another favourite that should be in every garden able to grow them. They are compact, typically reach 1 x 1m (3 x 3ft), and are incredibly free-flowering. Their small leaves and often gently arching habit allow them to mix happily with other shrubs, smaller perennials, and grasses or bulbs. Go for the large-flowered, extremely brightly coloured varieties such as *R.* 'Kirin' (Zone 7), if that is your preference, although there are some wonderfully refined older hybrids with delicate pastel flowers that are well worth searching for at garden centres or in catalogues from specialist nurseries.

Vibernum davidii

VIBURNUM

With a few exceptions, the viburnums are not really individually in the top-flight of ornamental shrubs but they can be grown on all soil types. That is not the same as saying they are boring, just that they are generally not flamboyant plants. Their charms tend to grow on you.

Some viburnum certainly do scale the heights of attraction when in flower: for example, the tiered *V. plicatum* 'Mariesii'(Zone 4) and the very similar *V.p.* 'Lanarth' (Zone 4) (both almost interchangeable in the gardening trade). These are shrubs for light shade and can reach 3 x 3m (10 x 10ft) if planted in suitable conditions and left unpruned. Alternatively, they can grow as low as 1m (3ft) with a spread of about 4m (12½ft) if the upward-growing shoots are removed each year after flowering.

For heavier shade there are some species of viburnum whose main attributes are their glossy evergreen foliage. *V. davidii* (Zone 6) in addition produces bright blue, egg-shaped berries if both male and female plants are planted fairly close to one another. It typically makes a compact bush 0.6 x 1m (2 x 3ft). The common laurustinus bush (*V. tinus*) (Zone 7) also tolerates quite deep shade, where it grows to about 2 x 2m (6½ x 6½ft) and forms a dense bush. It is especially useful as it can be hard-pruned, if necessary.

Pieris formosa var. forrestii

Perennials

Anemone nemorosa

ANEMONE

The most important anemone for shade gardening is the wood anemone (*A. nemorosa*) (Zone 4). Typically in mid-spring the flowers appear soon after the leaves in such numbers as to create solid pools of colour. In the wild, these are white, sometimes fading to pink, and occasionally lavender-blue. Many forms have been selected and there are now many for enthusiasts to choose from.

Wood anemone is not a plant for dark shade and will in fact disappear if it gets too overgrown. The flowers need light to open properly and will turn their faces to track the sun as it arches across the sky. My experience suggests they do not like heavy mulching, but in other gardens an annual fibrous mulch has been beneficial, so I recommend you proceed with caution.

A. nemorosa has many varieties, all of equal hardiness, and creates ever-widening clumps, reaching about 15cm (6in) in height at flowering time. *A.n.* 'Lady Doneraile' produces good white flowers; *A.n.* 'Robinsoniana' is a beautiful silvery lilac; the flower colour of *A.n.* 'Royal Blue' is self-explanatory; *A.n.* 'Bowles' Purple' has purple-flushed leaves on emerging;

and sweetly scented *A.n.* 'Buckland' is late flowering and has the biggest blooms.

There are other species superficially similar to the wood anemone such as *A. apennina* (Zone 6), which has more dissected leaves, a slightly taller stature – to 20cm (8in) – and flowers in blue or white. *A. ranunculoides* (Zone 4) bears bright yellow flowers and reaches to 25cm (10in). A hybrid between this and *A.nemorosa* is called *A.* x *lipsiensis* 'Pallida' (Zone 4), and it produces beautiful, pale yellow flowers.

Later in the season for half-shade sites there are taller species with branching heads of wood anemone-sized flowers, such as *A. rivularis* (Zone 6) with its purple-backed, white flowers. This clump-former grows 60–75cm (2–2½ft) high.

Later still, as summer heads into autumn, Japanese anemones (*A. hupehensis* and *A.* x *hybrida*) (Zone 4) start to open. These are gently spreading perennials 1m (3ft) high at flowering time, topped with sprays

Cardamine pentaphylla

of large, white or purple-pink flowers for many weeks. Japanese anemones are very suitable for light shade.

CARDAMINE

This genus of plants has "essence of woodland" writ large over it. Botanists have also reclassified it over recent years, and many species that used to be known as dentarias have now been renamed cardamines. I try to adapt, but truthfully it leaves my head spinning. One that has been left alone is lady's smock or cuckooflower (*C. pratensis*) (Zone 4). The specific name *pratensis* means "of meadows" and this is its more usual habitat, but it will grow in light shade as it prefers damp situations. It can flower in such numbers as to produce similar effects to pale lavender-blue phlox (*see picture on p.144*). It only grows 30cm (1ft) high, but can cover a wide area by self-seeding.

Other cardamines have a family likeness, as can be seen in *C. pentaphylla* (Zone 5) (*left*), this one being taller, up to 45cm (1½ft), and leafier than lady's smock. These other species are natural woodlanders so are very much at home in shady gardens. There are low-growing, white-flowered species such as *C. waldsteinii* (Zone 6) (which barely reaches 15cm/6in) as it slowly spreads and taller whites such as *C. heptaphylla* (Zone 6), which reaches 50cm (20in). A dark pink cardamine, *C. raphanifolia* (Zone 6), grows quite happily not only in ordinary well-drained soil but also in permanently wet soil alongside a stream. Its flower stems reach about 40cm (16in) high. This last species even crossed with *C. pratensis* to produce a hybrid we called 'Buckland' (Zone 5), which is like lady's smock on steroids and is also equally happy planted in water.

All the cardamines flower in spring and die down soon after flowering.

DACTYLORHIZA MARSH ORCHID

All of the hardy orchids in this genus are relatively easy to cultivate in your garden and most of them, as their common name suggests, are happy to grow near wet ground. However, their root tubers rot if planted in waterlogged soil and need to be in the aerated ground above water level. Fortunately, dactylorhizas do not demand the presence of permanent water as long as the root-run is cool, so woodland conditions are ideal.

The one hardy dactylorhiza that does not conform to these growing conditions is *D. fuchsii* (Zone 5), the native common spotted orchid of alkaline soils in the UK, especially the chalk downlands, but even this species quite happily settles down in gardens in cool conditions. It grows to 30cm (1ft).

The best species for your garden, and really in a league of their own for showiness, are *D. elata* (Zones 6–7) and Madeiran orchid (*D. foliosa*) (Zone 7). Both are similar, being clump-forming and growing to 60cm (2ft), but Madeiran orchid is perhaps more often encountered.

Surprisingly, coming from Madeira, it is hardy in the UK in an open, leafy soil in cool light shade. I have found it to be easy to cultivate with flower numbers doubling year on year. I have even seen Madeiran orchid in a friend's garden seeding into the crown of a marginal plant growing in their pond, so clearly it does not object to permanent moisture beneath its tubers.

DICENTRA BLEEDING HEART

This genus of plants is generally very easy to grow in sun or shade, although to me dicentras appear to be most at home in a woodland setting. The upright and then arching habit of one of the tall species, *D. spectabilis* (Zones 3–4), is typical of a woodland inhabitant. This species stays pretty much where put, gradually clumping up and reaching about 75cm (2½ft) high.

Virtually all of the other species and varieties of dicentra have a similar flower shape but on more compact plants, which typically spread by underground runners. This can be very welcome or quite alarming depending on the robustness of the neighbours you planted alongside.

Dicentra spectabilis

My advice would be not to plant any dicentra close to tiny treasured plants until you have grown it for a couple of years somewhere else to check on its spreading tendencies.

A few dicentras have grey-blue leaves. *D.* 'Langtrees' (Zone 5) is good in this respect; it also bears off-white flowers and has a running habit and a height of about 30cm (1ft). The more recent hybrid *D.* 'King of Hearts' (Zone 5) is more of a clump-former and produces beautiful flowers very like *D. spectabilis* but on a smaller plant – only growing 30cm (1ft) high. *D.* 'Bacchanal' (Zone 5) is a good red-pink variety, and *D.* 'Stuart Boothman' (Zone 5) has particularly feathery leaves and pink flowers. Both grow to 30cm (1ft) and spread by underground roots.

If you would like something a bit different, *D. macrantha* (Zone 4) reaches 75cm (2½ft) high and bears straw-yellow lockets. In woodland conditions, this species spreads gently by runners. *D. canadensis* and *D. cucullaria* (both Zone 3) (*see picture p.74*) are tiny treasures a few centimetres/inches high with white flowers. They should be grown with similar tiny tots where they can be appreciated without getting swamped.

EPIMEDIUM

In recent years, this group of plants has seen a meteoric rise in the number of new species in cultivation. Some 20 years ago there were perhaps 10 different species

Dactylorhiza foliosa

Epimedium x *versicolor* 'Sulphureum'

and varieties, which were mostly easy going perennials, grown for their subtle ground-covering foliage and sprays of spring flowers. They were perfect for edging borders in shady gardens. Now these stalwarts have been joined in cultivation by perhaps another 150 taxa, in a range of colours and forms that would have seemed unbelievable a few years ago.

E. x *versicolor* 'Sulphureum' (Zone 5) is as indispensable now as it always was. Its bronzed young leaves emerge in early spring, to 30cm (1ft) high, shortly before the sprays of primrose-yellow flowers open. The usually evergreen leaves need to be cut down just before the flowering shoots start to elongate in spring. This happens quite fast, so keep checking.

These same general cultivation facts also apply to other easy epimedium species such as *E.x warleyense* (Zone 5) (orange flowers), *E.* x *rubrum* (Zone 5) (red flowers), and *E. perralderianum* (Zone 7) (acid-yellow flowers).

The hybrid *E.* x *youngianum* (Zone 5) bears copper-coloured young leaves and sprays of spurred flowers in many shades of pink, purple, or white. The same characteristics and flower colours apply to the slightly taller, clump-forming *E. grandiflorum* (Zone 5), which has much bigger flowers and perhaps does better

outside in cooler, wetter areas (like the western side of the UK).

The recently introduced epimedium species flooding out of the Orient are simply mouthwatering. Many have gorgeously marbled young leaves and enormous spidery flowers.

EUPHORBIA SPURGE

Spurges can impart a frothy lightness to shady borders, and the many species and varieties are well worth experimenting with. Although some spurges are sun-lovers, others are very much at home in semi-shady gardens. Their flowers are typically yellow or yellow-green but can be orange. They are held in distinctive spurge-fashion, as shown in the photograph (*below*). Some euphorbias also have beautifully coloured young growths, which usually fade to green as the season progresses.

After retreating underground through winter, *E. griffithii* 'Fireglow' (Zone 6) produces both purple young growth and orange flower heads on 50cm (20in) stems for many weeks in spring. By mid-summer the plant, which grows readily in sun or shade, has reached about 1m (3ft) high and has assumed

Euphorbia griffithii 'Fireglow'

an almost shrub-like form. Finally in autumn the leaves are transformed into shades of yellow and orange before dying. The inexorable increase in girth of the clump needs to be watched either by planting suitably robust neighbours such as tall hostas or by being prepared to remove spreading underground shoots around the edge of the clump in late winter.

Geranium sylvaticum

The evergreen wood spurge (*E. amygdaloides*) (Zone 6) is ideal for shady conditions. In *E.a.* 'Purpurea' (Zone 6) the leaves and stems are strongly flushed purple-red, which contrasts attractively with the greeny yellow flowers. Both mature to about 40cm (16in) high with a similar spread and are clump-forming, but they do self-seed. *E. amygdaloides* var. *robbiae* (Zone 7) differs in having a running habit and more rounded leaves. It reaches up to 60cm (2ft) high.

GERANIUM CRANESBILL

Except for the alpine cranesbills, nearly all other cranesbill are suitable for light shade and are excellent for creating a wild or natural "feel" to shady borders. I remember many years ago seeing a large new garden carved out under 6m (20ft) high trees, in which the vast majority of the planting was *G. x oxonianum* (Zone 4) varieties and other geranium species. Very good it looked too.

In half-shade the 80cm (32in) high, clump-forming *G. psilostemon* (Zone 6) is spectacular in early summer with its magenta-crimson, dark-eyed flowers, and it is about this time of year that *G. x oxonianum* in its numerous forms starts to flower. Some varieties, such as salmon-pink *G. x o.* 'Wageningen' just keep flowering all summer, whereas others tail off after a month or so. If cut back to the ground at this point, they rapidly grow more foliage and can often flower again later in the season. Most reach about 30cm (1ft) high, with an individual spread of about 90cm (3ft).

Two cranesbill naturally growing in woods are *G. maculatum* (Zone 4), with its cool lavender-pink flowers in late spring, and *G. sylvaticum* (Zone 4), with its blue flowers that gently self seed. Both mature to 60cm (2ft) high, are clump-forming, and have lovely white forms. *G. pratense* (Zone 5) is similar but taller – up to 90cm (3ft) – and flowers later in the season.

Earlier, in late spring, *G. macrorrhizum* (Zone 4) covers itself with pink or white flowers on dense, weed-suppressing clumps, 30cm (1ft) high, of aromatic leaves. This species can even tolerate dry shade.

Mourning widow (*G. phaeum*) (Zone 5) survives in dense shade, forming erect clumps 60cm (2ft) high. Its reflexing dark maroon flowers are more "quiet charm" than "spectacular".

HELLEBORUS LENTEN ROSES

Perhaps more than any other perennial, hellebores embody the spirit of woodland or shade gardening in springtime. Their flowers seem almost impervious to the weather, more often than not bouncing back from frosts, which leave them dejected and prostrate on the ground. Their dark green foliage is a perfect foil for the more usual fresh yellow-greens of many of the emerging leaves at this time of year, and their 45cm (1½ft) domed outline mixes

Helleborus x hybridus

happily with most plant combinations to be found in a woodland garden.

Thanks to dedicated breeding work by growers around the world, but especially in the UK by Helen Ballard, Elizabeth Strangman, John Massey (Ashwood nursery), and Robin White (Blackthorn nursery), there are now a wide range of colours and forms of lenten rose (*H. x hybridus*) (Zone 5) readily available. Seed strains have been dramatically improved, and flower colours range from white through pink to almost red, with blues, yellows, and picotee-edged, and all of these can be spotted inside or not. More expensive to buy are the doubles and semi-doubles. These too are improving enormously both in form and vigour. Because these flower types are mostly self-sterile, their flower heads can remain looking good for longer than single-flowered strains.

I have never found that the large, white flowered Christmas rose (*H. niger*) (Zone 5) grows particularly well in the garden, but I am sure it does much better on limey soils.

A hellebore that does tolerate more shade than most is *H. foetidus* (Zone 5). This has attractive, fingered, dark green leaves making clumps 50cm (20in) high and wide. It produces airy sprays of green flowers, picotee-edged in purple.

HOSTA PLAINTAIN LILY

These very bold-foliaged plants should be used with discretion if a balanced composition is to be achieved (*see pp.122–4*). Leaf size can vary from a few centimetres/inches to more than 30cm (1ft) in length, and the foliage colour from plain

green, blue, or gold to silver- and gold-variegated. Hosta flowers range from white to rich purple. *H. crispula* (Zone 4) is typical of the larger-growing variegated types, which eventually form clumps nearly 80cm (32in) high. It tends not to flower very freely.

Choice of varieties will obviously be a matter of personal taste, as will the decision whether to protect the plants against slugs and snails, because these creatures have a passionate taste for hosta. Personally I do spread slug pellets but usually only in the very early spring when the hosta buds are just beginning to swell, because damage at this bud stage from slug-munching results in some very tatty leaves later as they unfurl.

Since I grow hostas primarily for the effects of their spring and early summer foliage, when their various textures and colours are so strong, these are the seasons that I want to see them pristine and undamaged from slugs. Later in the year, in areas where many spring-flowering plants have been concentrated in shady areas, I do not mind sharing my hostas with the indigenous wildlife.

Most hostas grow in sun or shade but definitely prefer a cool soil especially in brighter positions. A general rule of thumb is that in full sun you get more flowers and more compact plants; and in shade there will be fewer flowers on taller stems, and larger leaves.

Hosta crispula

MECONOPSIS

This genus includes the wonderful blue poppies (such as *M. betonicifolia*) (Zone 7) of China and Nepal, but these are not the only ones. There are other species from the Orient, which have yellow, white, pink, and even red flowers. None of them could truthfully be classified as very easy to grow.

The one species that can be readily cultivated is Welsh poppy (*M. cambrica*) (Zone 6). This 40cm (16in) high native to northern Europe and Britain has yellow or orange flowers and fresh green, ferny foliage. It self-seeds freely in cool, half-shady spots. For this reason it is welcomed by some gardeners and disliked by others, so perhaps it would be wise to see which camp you fall into before introducing it to your garden. There is no doubt it can be a bit too much of a good thing even for devotees, but a sharp twist when grasping leaves and stems will break it off at ground level, preventing seeding and allowing the root to rapidly re-shoot.

If only the blue poppies were as easy to cultivate. These form clumps of grey, felted leaves which send up erect flowering stems to 1m (3ft) high. For many years The Garden House was renowned for its stands of blue poppies, and the secret of their success was partly the high rainfall and

Meconopsis betonicifolia

partly the soil preparation prior to planting. Copious amounts of well-rotted manure were added to the north, sloping bank on which they grew. Regular watering and cool conditions on the run-up to flowering in late spring seemed to be essential to get the best and purest blue colour.

Most blue poppies do not set viable seed, but *M.* 'Lingholm' (Zone 5) does, and the development of this strain has meant that strong young plants are becoming much easier to obtain.

OMPHALODES

Plants in this small genus in the forget-me-not family look somewhat like a perennial forget-me-not. There are two species especially relevant to the shade gardener. These are *O. verna* (Zone 6) and *O. cappadocica* (Zone 6), both of which bear sprays of pure blue flowers in spring.

O. verna has a more vigorous running habit and should be grown with caution close to frailer neighbours. It is, though, the hardier of the two species, is only a few centimetres/inches high, and grows even in dry shade. *O.v.* var. *grandiflora* is the best one to cultivate. There is also a white variety.

O. cappadocica is more clump-forming, spreading more slowly by stoloniferous roots, and can suffer cold damage in winter, especially if planted in an exposed site where wind chill is more pronounced. It is also taller, reaching 20cm (8in) high. It creates pools of pure rich blue flowers and so is more ornamental than *O. verna*. A selection by Helen Dillon in Ireland, called *O. cappadocica* 'Starry Eyes', has this blue reduced to the centre of the petals with very pale blue, almost white edges, and is well-named. It has a similar size and hardiness to its blue parent.

PHLOX

To many gardeners, the name phlox will be linked with the border perennials, which are such a mid-summer mainstay of traditional herbaceous beds and borders, or else with the alpine evergreen species, *P. subulata* and *P. douglasii*, which are so

Omphalodes verna

indispensable for rockeries. However, both groups need full sun.

Fortunately, there is a less well-known group of phlox, including *P. divaricata* (Zone 4) and *P. stolonifera* (zone 4), which contains shade-lovers, woodland plants by natural inclination, which are best in cool conditions. Both species flower in late spring or early summer. *P. divaricata* is the taller of the two, having flower stems reaching 30–45cm (1–1½ft); it also has a more sprawling habit. There are numerous varieties with flowers ranging from white through lavender-blue to purple, and some are beautifully scented, like *C.d.* 'Clouds of Perfume'. Other varieties that I have found to be reliable are *C.d.* 'Dirigo Ice', *C.d.* 'Blue Dreams', and *C.d.* 'May Breeze'. All are similar in size, habit, and hardiness to the type species. *C.* 'Chattahoochee' (Zone 4) bears lavender-blue flowers with a striking purple eye, but appears to be a bit more tricky to keep growing well.

P. stolonifera has more prostrate stems than *P. divaricata*, rooting as they go and quickly forming large patches. It needs a cool, semi-shady spot as it can suffer in full sun. Flower colour is similar to the range found in *P. divaricata*, but the flower heads

Phlox divaricata 'May Breeze'

Pleione formosana

are more compact and held closer to the ground, at about 20cm (8in).

PLEIONE & OTHER GROUND ORCHIDS

Pleiones are often called windowsill orchids because they seem quite amenable to cultivation in pots there. A few species, however, grow outside if they can be accommodated in the right spot. Their main problem is not cold temperatures but dislike of winter wet, so a place that is perhaps overhung by sheltering evergreen leaves or on the leeward side of a tree trunk is worth seeking out. In pleiones grown under cover, the swollen pseudobulbs should normally be planted at or just above soil level in the container, but if you are trying some pleiones outside you should plant them a little deeper so these pseudoulbs are covered by soil.

P. formosana (Zone 8 if dry in winter) is only about 15cm (6in) high in flower and forms large patches in its native woods, where it flourishes in loose, leaf litter. Therefore an open, free-draining medium should be created if trying it outside. *P. bulbocodioides* (Zone 7) is similar in size and cultivation requirements but has more pink and red in the fringed labellum. It

slowly increases in girth through the addition of new pseudobulbs.

There are other ground orchids that are ideal for shady spots. Slipper orchids (*Cypripedium*) are perhaps the most instantly recognizable. They are all expensive to buy, so cultivation in pots is more often considered a safer option than in the open ground. If you do fall for their charms and want to grow them outside I would recommend you prepare the ground well (see p. 93). Typically slipper orchids are clump-forming, only 15cm (6in) high, and are very slow to increase.

The rather less flamboyant calanthes and epipactis also grow well outside in well-prepared beds and borders. These two genera have flowers in upright spikes, 30–40cm (12–16in) high, and have a more exotic resemblance to the native UK helleborines (*Epipactis*).

PRIMULA PRIMROSE

Common primrose (*P. vulgaris*) (Zone 5) is just one of more than 200 primula species worldwide, but it has spawned many dozens of different varieties over the years. Since micro-propagation became common currency, double primroses have enjoyed a bit of a renaissance. At their best, these doubles completely cover themselves in

Primula whitei

flower. Regular division after flowering every two or three years and replanting in fresh ground are advisable. They reach 15cm (6in) high.

P. sieboldii (Zone 5) is an excellent easy primrose for shade, 30cm (1ft) high in flower, and slowly spreading by rhizomes. In Japan, it can grow in hay meadows in the wild, and it has also long been revered there as a garden plant. Many varieties have been selected. *P. sieboldii* dies completely away soon after flowering in early summer.

P. whitei (Zone 5) is one of the petiolarid group of primulas which overwinters as a large bud. In spring this bud enlarges to a posy of exquisite powder-blue flowers with leaves and stems covered in a dusting of silver farina. The overwintering bud is susceptible to scratching birds and too much water, so planting on a slope in a cool place, perhaps under an overhanging rhododendron, is a good idea. *P. whitei* reaches 10cm (4in) high.

In damp, semi-shady corners of the garden, Asiatic primulas should be high on the list of inhabitants. These bog primulas are best in permanently damp soils but still grow if the site is just cool. Many of this group have a candelabra arrangement with flowers in tiered whorls and can be

found in orange, purple, and yellow as well as many other colours. Alternatively you could have a quieter planting scheme and use cowslips (*P. veris*) (Zone 5) in a damp spot. These grow only up to 20cm (8in) in height.

PULMONARIA LUNGWORT

In clubs and societies there is often a hardcore of people who do the bulk of the necessary work and, because they do not shout about it, they are very frequently overlooked and almost taken for granted. Pulmonarias, I feel, are my gardening equivalent. They are great garden plants but I take them for granted, growing as they do in almost any soil, in any position, in shade or sun. This indifference probably stems from 35 years ago, when I started gardening, and the only common pulmonaria was *P. officinalis* (Zone 4), with its rather dowdy spotted leaves and pink flowers fading to dirty blue.

Since that time this genus has enjoyed a revival of fortune, and there are around 150 varieties to choose from. There are now pulmonarias with all-silver leaves (*P.* 'Cotton Cool'; Zone 5), dark royal blue flowers (*P.* 'Blue Ensign'; Zone 5), through all shades between to very pale blue (*P.* 'Opal'; Zone 5) and many whites. All show no sign of pink and make clumps of leaves some 30cm (1ft) high by 45cm (1½ft) wide. Pink flowers were not ignored, though, and there are now clean-coloured varieties ranging from palest blush to nearly red, and all without a hint of blue.

If most pulmonarias' broadly oval leaves are a bit ordinary for your tastes, you could opt for the beautifully marked, narrow foliage of *P. longifolia* (Zone 5), which has heads of smaller flowers in very dark blue. This is a slightly smaller plant attaining 20 x 30cm (8 x 12in), and it carries its flowers rather more elegantly.

All the pulmonarias are wonderful at growing beneath deciduous shrubs, where in the glow of spring sunshine they can strut their recently acquired clean colours, before retiring to anonymity, out of sight below the shrubs' leaves.

SAXIFRAGA

This is a huge genus where the majority of sections are sun-lovers. It is also one in which the botanists are busy changing plant names, hopefully not to something else again by the time you read this.

Two that are at home in full shade are *S. stolonifera* and *S.* 'Cuscutiformis' (both Zone 6). These spread, as does the houseplant mother-of-thousands variety, by fine runners rooting when they touch the ground. They both have nicely marbled leaves and airy sprays of white flowers, to 30cm (1ft) high, on red stems. Both will quickly cover a square metre of ground.

Another group of easy, spreading saxifrages that are happy in half-shade are the "mossy" ones. However, they are sometimes damaged by birds (*see p.67*). No such problem exists with London pride (*S.* x *urbium*) (Zone 6), which is very useful as an edging plant in poor, shady conditions, as is its more refined offspring, *S.* 'Clarence Elliott' (Zone 6), which bears sprays of pretty pink flowers. Both form dense, dark green carpets of foliage about 10cm (4in) high and have branching flower stalks up to 30cm (1ft) and 20cm (8in), respectively.

The last group of shade-loving saxifrages to flower are members of the "fortunei" group. These make clumps of foliage looking more like heucheras to the uninitiated, except with fleshy leaves. In early autumn, or occasionally even later, they send up sprays of usually white flowers, often on red stems, to 30cm (1ft). These are worth the wait. *S.* 'Rubrifolia' (Zone 6) has brown-red leaves that are rich red-purple on

Saxifraga stolonifera

Smilacina racemosa

the underside. It forms clumps 20 x 30cm (8 x 12in). *S.* 'Mount Nachi' (Zone 7) is similar but much dwarfer (only 15cm/6in high in flower) and later flowering (late autumn with me). I have grown *S.* 'Rosea' (Zone 5) for years and it produces beautiful, clean pink flowers in early summer in sprays 20–30cm (8–12in) high, above clumps of fresh green, rounded leaves. Other varieties are being introduced all the time, because this group has been a firm favourite with the Japanese for many years.

SMILACINA FALSE SOLOMON'S SEAL

These are common plants of the woods of North America and the Orient. Not surprisingly, given their common name of false solomon's seas, smilacinas resemble solomon's seals, except for their broader leaves. The two species that have been in cultivation for a long time are both American. One, *S. racemosa* (Zone 4), would be high on any list I was making for perennials suitable for growing in shade, not least for the gorgeous lemony scent of its flowers. Most of the plants I have seen in cultivation reach about 60cm (2ft) high but will be even taller in richer, shadier spots. *S. racemosa* can follow its flowers with attractive berries of bright orange-red, which in some seasons can be quite a feature. It has an arching habit and slowly spreads by its roots.

As more exploring is done in the Orient, especially by plant collectors such as Dan

Pulmonaria officinalis

Hinkley from America and Bleddyn and Sue Wynn-Jones from Crug Farm in Wales, so more of these false solomon's seals are being introduced. Some are taller, up to 2.4m (8ft) high in the case of *S. oleracea* (Zone 6), creating dramatic seasonal changes in the landscape of woodland perennial plantings. This species produces large purple-pink flowers with white picotee-edged backs to the petals. Still rare in gardens, it remains to be seen how it will perform generally in cultivation. I have even seen a purple-foliaged form of this species in Dan Hinkley's garden in Washington State, which was quite stunning.

THALICTRUM MEADOW RUE

The thalictrums include some very valuable plants for light shade and range in height from just a few centimetres up to 2.4m (8ft). Despite their native haunts frequently being meadows, in the garden thalictrums do not look out of place in a semi-shaded location. They all have fluffy lilac flowers with yellow stamens in airy heads, unless otherwise mentioned.

Among those that positively demand half-shade are the miniature *T. kiusianum* (Zone 5) which has attractive ferny leaves. It grows only 20cm (8in) high and gently runs in loose, woody soil. *T. kiusianum* should be planted with other little treasures because it is not very robust.

Taller-growing – to about 30cm (1ft) – is *T. tuberosum* (Zone 5), which produces

Thalictrum rochebruneanum

sprays of larger white flowers. Again it prefers an open, friable soil and gently runs. Taller yet again is the large-flowered (for a thalictrum) *T. diffusiflorum* (Zone 5) with 2.5cm (1in) wide flowers. However, it is not very robust, and produces only frail flowering stems, 60cm (2ft) high, which tend to flop over. More robust is the even taller *T. chelidonii* (Zone 5), which grows to more than 1m (3ft) and has attractive maidenhair-like foliage, as do so many of the meadow rues. None of the last three mentioned species will run, and none increases in girth very much.

Two of the highest thalictrums are *T. rochebruneanum* (Zone 5) and *T. delavayii* (Zone 5). *T. rochebruneanum* produces robust, purple-flushed flowering stems and reaches about 2m (6½ft). In my experience, it prefers a partially shady spot. By contrast, *T. delavayii* seems just as happy and stays more compact in full sun as long as its root-run is cool. In a shady location it can grow to 2.4m (8ft) high, although it is also prone to flopping under its own weight. Both species are non-running clump-formers with only a handful of erect flowering stems emerging from the root, even when established.

For thalictrums to plant in light shade or nearly full sun, I would suggest *T. aquilegiifolium* (Zone 5), which has purple-pink or white flowers in late spring. It attains 1.5m (5ft) in height and produces broader clumps than those species already mentioned, as well as many more flowering stems, which support each other rather more effectively. The glaucous-leaved *T. flavum* subsp *glaucum* (Zone 5) bears pale yellow flowers in early summer on 2m (6½ft) high stems. Both these species carry their flowers in dense, domed heads at the tops of the flowering stems.

VERATRUM

Among perennials, rodgersias, rheums, hostas, and veratrums create bold foliage effects in woodland conditions. However, unlike the others named, veratrums manage to do this in an upright form. The effect is rather like a mullein (*Verbascum*), with

Veratrum viride

ribbed, broad, dark green leaves. The flowers when they come in summer are in a branched spike with small, starry flowers. New plantings may take several years before they choose to flower.

Veratrums require a cool, rich soil. Although in the wild they tend to grow in open meadows or woodland glades, in cultivation they are best planted in some shade to keep the foliage looking healthy. They start to develop very early in the year, and like hostas are prone to slug damage at such a time. I have found them to be painfully slow to establish, but once they have they are a constant source of pride and enjoyment. Patience is definitely needed for these plants.

All veratrum species grow to about 1.5m (5ft) high and are basically similar with handsome, prominently veined leaves and architectural flower spikes differing really only in flower colour. In *V. album* (Zone 5) they are white, *V. viride* (Zone 5) green, and *V. nigrum* (Zone 6) maroon/purple-black.

V. maackii (Zone 6) produces narrower, less glossy leaves and more open, elegant flowers and is perhaps less dramatic than the other species mentioned. Generally, it is an easier plant to mix successfully within a woodland garden than the other species.

Bulbs

ARISAEMA

Arisaemas are an acquired taste as many are quite sombre in colouring, which, together with their mottled stems and hooded flowers, lend them a slightly sinister air. I just love them, especially the more prolifically mottled species. There are about 150 species, mostly growing in woods in eastern Asia (more than 40 species in Japan alone), and when planted in your garden will impart a little eastern exoticism to shady spots.

All arisaemas have the same basic structure as *A. sazensoo* (Zone 6), which is 45cm (1½ft) high, but there can be variation in the different elements making up the various species. Some species such as the North American native *A. triphyllum* (Zone 3) reach only about 30cm (1ft) high and have striped green "flowers" or spathes almost hidden among the foliage. They are good for naturalizing where space is not too an issue because they seed themselves around. Other species such as *A. nepenthoides* (Zone 5) can reach 1.5m (5ft) in height. It bears striped and spotted purple and white spathes. Individually none

Arisaema sazensoo

of the species takes up any room as they are all so strongly upright.

Arisaema spathes can be held below the foliage at ground level or well above the leaves, the stems can be mottled or plain, the leaves silver-splashed or plain green, and the spathe colour can vary from green, yellow, and pink to dark purple, and may be striped.

If I were restricted to just one arisaema it would be *A. ciliatum* var. *liubaense* (Zone 7), which is easy to cultivate and grows to 60cm (2ft). The slim, elegant spathes are dark purple and white borne on mottled stems, and are produced in such numbers as to resemble a troupe of ever-alert meerkats standing on guard duty. With time, it produces a colony of widely spaced "sentries" 30cm (1ft) square.

CORYDALIS

Although this genus comprises bulbs and perennials, it has been included here for simplicity. Its overground shoots, leaves, and flowers all bear a strong visual similarity. The plants nearly all have ferny leaves, a typically compact habit, and sprays of flowers ranging in colour from white, pink, and yellow to blue.

The most important bulbous species for the shade gardener is *C. solida* (Zone 6), which is very easy to grow in the open garden, yet intricate and small enough at 20cm (8in) high to be an excellent small container plant as well. Of the many cultivars, terracotta-red *C.s.* subsp. *solida* 'George Baker' (Zone 6) takes some beating, but is less robust and very much slower to increase than the type.

Not many years ago, the only two blue-flowered corydalis were hard to find, difficult to grow, and expensive to buy. Then *C. flexuosa* (Zone 5) was introduced and within a handful of years its ease of propagation and cultivation made it a common garden-centre plant. This, and

Corydalis curviflora subsp. *rosthornii*

the selections from it, make clumps of ferny leaves 15cm (6in) high and perhaps 30cm (1ft) across, above which hover the sprays of flowers to 30cm (1ft) high. *C.f.* 'China Blue', which was one of the original introduced varieties, still holds its own among the many selections made since. *C.f.* 'Balang Mist' bears very pale blue flowers.

Other species with blue flowers have since become available. For example, *C. elata* (Zone 6), which is slightly less spreading and taller, at 45cm (1½ft), than *C. flexuosa*, and glaucous-leaved *C. curviflora* subsp. *rosthornii* (Zone 7). The latter makes clumps of glaucous leaves 15 x 20cm (6 x 8in) topped by exquisite blue flowers on red stems, to 25cm (10in).

There are also yellow, white, and lavender-blue corydalis species, some of which are scented, but your appreciation or otherwise of these plants, especially when planted en masse, may depend on your attitude towards self-seeding. Some species spread by quite prolific seeding, but this should not put you off because the seedlings are very easy to pull out.

Cyclamen hederifolium

CYCLAMEN

This is a wonderful group of plants for well-drained soils in shade. The mostly hardy cyclamen species are perfect for growing under trees and shrubs, where the shading plants' roots suck up excess moisture.

The easiest to grow and the best garden cyclamen is *C. hederifolium* (Zone 5), at 10cm (4in) high. Its corms can grow to the diameter of a dinner plate and its leaves to 15cm (6in) across. More often they are smaller than this, however. The first sign of this plant, usually in late summer, is the odd white or pink flower peeking out from the shade. For this reason, I like to cover the ground where *C. hederifolium* grows with a leaf mould-based mulch, to create a better background for the flowers. By early autumn the number of blooms on each corm can be many dozen, and the leaves will be starting to emerge. The colour range of this foliage can be anything from almost plain green to entirely silver, with beautifully mottled and marbled variations in between. The leaves remain all through winter, long after the flowers have faded, before dying away in spring.

Barely growing 10cm (4in) high, *C. coum* (Zone 5) is the other readily available cyclamen, capable of creating beautiful patches of colour with its pink,

carmine, or white flowers in early spring. It is not generally as easy to establish as *C. hederifolium* but is more colourful in flower, associating really well with late snowdrops and early crocus. Less easy still to cultivate is *C. repandum* (Zone 7), which seems to appreciate more shade. It produces its carmine-red flowers, 15cm (6in) high, later in spring.

ERYTHRONIUM FAWN LILY

When in flower, these aristocratic lily-like bulbs range in height from 10cm (4in) to 40cm (16in). The flowers can be pink, white, or yellow, and are held either singly or up to five on a stem (more in rare cases) above a pair of oval leaves at ground level. The leaves are plain green or variously mottled with silver and purple.

Most of the species grow wild in the states of the Pacific north-west of the USA, where the climate is cool in spring but dry in summer. Such conditions are important for some species. *E. revolutum* (Zone 5), however, is not too fussy and has adapted to garden conditions very well, especially in areas of high rainfall. It has pink flowers on 20cm (8in) stems and self-seeds if the ground is undisturbed and not overgrown. *E. californicum* (of gardens) (Zone 5) is of

similar height with creamy white flowers and white anthers. *E. tuolumnense* (Zone 5) has plain green leaves and bright yellow flowers in multi-headed spikes, up to 45cm (1½ft) high, rapidly clumping up but not seeding. *E. dens-canis* (Zone 3) is a native of southern Europe and is only 15cm (6in) high with pink or white flowers and handsome foliage.

From eastern North America, a similar-sized erythronium except with yellow flowers is *E. americanum* (Zone 2), but this species in the wild and in gardens can be shy-flowering. Of the many other very desirable species, most require a little more care than those mentioned.

Hybrid erythroniums clump up more quickly than species ones, and once established produce many flowers. Look out particularly for *E.* 'Pagoda' (primrose-yellow); *E.* 'White Beauty'; *E.* 'Joanna' (pink/yellow); *E.* 'Jeanette Brickell' (white); *E.* 'Rosalind' (pink/white); and *E.* 'Janice' (pink). All are Zone 5 hardiness and reach about 30cm (1ft) high when in flower.

GALANTHUS SNOWDROP

Snowdrops are bulbs for deciduous shade. They are able to cope with full shade during summer, but need light during winter and early spring, when most of them flower. Snowdrops are also happy to grow where there is no shade, especially on north-facing slopes, which are slightly cooler.

To snowdrop enthusiasts the variations in flower shape, the amount and distribution of green present on the inner petals, and a host of other minutiae are

Erythronium dens-canis

Galanthus nivalis

endlessly fascinating and have resulted in a bewildering number of named forms. I fall into the category of interested bystander, growing those varieties and species that seem obviously distinctive, particularly those that look good from my standing height and are good doers. Fortunately, these limitations do not restrict my choice too much. With a little thought, a succession of these pristine flowers can be enjoyed for several months.

Among the singles, I can recommend G. 'S. Arnott' (broad, rounded petals); G. 'Magnet' (long, thin flower stalks so the flowers tremble in a breeze); G. 'Merlin' (big flowers with solid green marks on the inner petals); G. plicatus 'Wendy's Gold' (yellow petal markings); and G. 'Straffan' (late flowering and sometimes carrying more than one flower on a stem). All grow to 15–20cm (6–8in) high and are hardy down to Zone 4.

As for doubles, G. 'Barbara's Double' and G. 'Hippolyta' (both Zone 4) are good, with near-perfect, green centres to well-shaped outer petals. G. 'Hippolyta' is the taller, reaching 20cm (8in), perhaps twice the height of G. 'Barbaras Double'.

Among the species, G. reginae-olgae (Zone 7) is distinctive in that it flowers in autumn; in nearly all other respects it is identical to common snowdrop (G. nivalis) (Zone 4). Both grow 10cm (4in) high.

LILIUM LILY

The natural home of many lily species is the woodland glade or wood margins, and all look right in a garden environment in dappled light. The old adage often applied to clematis of "feet in shade, heads in sun"

applies to lilies as well. The one thing the vast majority of lilies demand, though, is good drainage. The bulbs will rot if grown where standing water is present.

I have tried to avoid overwet problems by planting some lilies on banks in moisture-retentive soil where surplus water naturally drains away. This was a particular success with one of the queens of lily species, L. auratum (Zone 5), which in its natural habitat in Japan grows in perfectly drained volcanic ash. Its huge white flowers on 2m (6½ft) high stems have a central stripe of yellow, leading to its common name of golden-ray lily. It gives off the most intoxicatingly sweet fragrance for weeks in late summer.

Some lilies naturalize by self-seeding in light woodland, and prime among these would be L. martagon (Zone 4), which has 1.5m (5ft) high stems carrying widely spaced, downward-facing flowers of purple-pink or white with strongly reflexing petals. Its flower shape and arrangement are typical of a range of lilies such as the similar-sized L. hansonii (Zone 6) with its orange flowers; the two species readily hybridize (as illustrated).

There are also trumpet-shaped lilies and those with branching heads of upward-facing flowers. They all come in a wide range of colours and are relatively inexpensive to buy. Groups of three or five are unsurpassed as container plants.

A hybrid of *Lilium martagon*, almost certainly with *L. hansonii.*

Narcissus 'Hawera'

NARCISSUS DAFFODIL

One of the most natural places to see daffodils growing in a garden setting is in the light shade of an established orchard or in thin woodland such as where lent daffodil (*N. pseudonarcissus*) (Zone 5) flourishes in the wild. Lent daffodils and Tenby daffodils (*N. obvallaris*) (Zone 5) actually take some beating for naturalizing, even in thin grass. Both grow no taller than 30cm (1ft). Daffodils are not plants for dense shade, though, and the more light they have the better they flower.

The bigger the scale of the available space at your disposal, the better the taller-growing varieties of daffodil will look. However, I prefer the charms and scale of the smaller-growing types, where their foliage is hardly an eyesore as it dies back. The "cyclamineus" hybrids are especially good for creating natural effects in small to medium-sized gardens, even though the frequent self-seeding so vital for creating wild effects is not available, because these hybrids are sterile. Many of the "cyclamineus" hybrids are 30–45cm (1–1½ft) tall and so mix beautifully with a whole range of similarly sized or smaller woodlanders. The choice of hybrids is large and mainly a matter of personal taste, but I still favour 30cm (1ft) high *N.* 'February Gold' (Zone 6).

Among smaller daffodils, the 20cm (8in) high *N.* 'Hawera' (Zone 6) grows and flowers in light shade, although it does prefer a sunnier, better-drained spot – as befits its *N. triandrus* parent. *N. cyclamineus* (Zone 6) with its distinctive, fully reflexing flowers on 15cm (6in) stems is quite happy in damper positions and will self-seed if the conditions suit it.

TRILLIUM WAKE ROBIN

It is sometimes hard to work out why some plants achieve almost cult-like status while others with similar charms are almost overlooked. There is no doubt, though, that wake robins enjoy the former, elevated position. Their upright then spreading habit, strong leaf shape, and large prominent flowers are attributes of many shrubs, notably rhododendrons, and so perhaps entitle wake robins (along with arisaemas) to "honorary shrub" status.

The sheltered conditions between shrubs in traditional woodland gardens are ideal for wake robins, too, providing both shade and wind protection. The bigger-leaved species in particular become a little ragged in exposed sites.

T. grandiflorum (Zone 5) is one of the best for gardens. It bears large, white flowers, fading to pink, on stems up to 45cm (1½ft) high. It is pushed close for top spot by *T. chloropetalum* (Zone 6) with its sessile flowers sitting on top of the large, rounded ruff of leaves that can reach 60 x 60cm (2 x 2ft). Similar-flowered *T. kurabayashii* (Zone 6) also attracts high levels of envy-enducement with its beautifully marked foliage. It grows to 30cm (1ft) high.

Trillium grandiflorum

Grasses and Bamboos

ANEMANTHELE PHEASANT'S TAIL GRASS

This is a genus with just a single species, *A. lessoniana* (Zone 8). The grass itself has undergone three name changes since I first started growing it, which is no real problem except that I have been tempted by enticing catalogue descriptions and bought it three times. Such actions have been made all the more galling because the original plant had seeded itself all over the garden! Whatever its name, it is a beautiful grass.

Its narrow leaves form arching clumps, perhaps 45 x 45 cm (1½ x 1½ft) high, with red-brown tints by mid-season. In late summer, long graceful flower stems arch up and then cascade down under their own weight, creating a haze of soft pink and brown. Pheasant's tail grass is sensational when covered in glistening dew in early morning autumn light, and stays looking good for a long time.

To keep the grass looking tidy, trim it back to about 30cm (1ft) in late winter, before the new leaves start to expand. Although it self-seeds readily, this is not really a problem because the seedlings are surface rooting and easily pulled out.

Pheasant's tail grass is easy to cultivate on heavy or loamy soils. It grows satisfactorily in half-shade, but its best colour develops in better light conditions. I try to site this grass on the tops of banks,

Anemanthele lessoniana

where the cascading flowers can best be displayed and where the light can stream through them.

BAMBOOS BAMBOO

Due to bamboo name changes, many of the arundinarias are now scattered through other genera. Two very useful species at home in shade, for example, have moved to *Fargesia* and these are *F. nitida* (Zone 4) and *F. murielae* (Zone 4). In hot climates these species demand shade, but in the cooler UK they are equally happy in full sun. Both are clump-formers, very slowly spreading at the root and producing canes 3–4m (10–12½ft) in height as well as billowing masses of narrow green leaves. The clumps of both species will increase in girth by about 6cm (2½in) a year. Their canes too are narrow and very tightly packed – green coloured in the case of *F. murielae* and black and glossy on *F. nitida*. Both these fargesias need plenty of space above them to grow properly, but they can create very elegant screening and shelter in shady conditions.

Pleioblastus viridistriatus (formerly *Arundinaria viridistriata*) (Zone 5) is an altogether smaller bamboo. It sends up thin canes up to 1m (3ft) in height, which can be cut to the ground annually, resulting in more brightly coloured yellow leaves. It is very useful for creating patches of bright variegated foliage in shade, but it does run, so is likely to be anti-social among less robust plants. The clump increases in diameter by as much as 45cm (1½ft) a year when established. There is also a silver-variegated species, *P. variegatus* (Zone 5), of similar size, with the same attributes and faults. For contained beds or container-growing, both species are extremely suitable, and are usefully restricted in width by the container's dimensions.

A very vigorous bamboo is *Sasa veitchii* (Zone 6), a shade-lover whose

Pleioblastus viridistriatus

leaves wither at the edges, giving the appearance of being variegated. Be warned, however, I have seen the roots of this bamboo going 2m (6½ft) deep and running 3m (10ft) horizontally. This handsome foliage plant could be grown in a container standing on a plastic saucer, so those roots cannot escape.

CAREX SEDGE

This is a huge genus containing more than 1,000 species, many of which flourish in damp habitats in the wild. Sedges are not very exciting in flower, so they are mostly cultivated in gardens for their foliage.

The thread-like, narrow leaves of the bronze-leaved species from New Zealand, such as *C. buchananii* (Zone 7), *C. comans* (Zone 7), and *C. testacea* (Zone 6), are normally recommended for sun, but I have seen them used very effectively in shady sites. All three make domed mounds 45 x 45cm (1½ x 1½ft). Of similar size and habit is the green counterpart to these New Zealand species, *C. albula* (Zone 7), sometimes called frosted curls, which

Carex elata 'Aurea'

appears almost grey from a distance and so is useful for introducing colour contrast.

The variegated sedges are well catered for among shade-lovers. One of the brightest in spring is Bowles' golden grass (*C. elata* 'Aurea') (Zone 5), which is able to grow in water but does not demand it. When planted in full sun, its young leaves are some of the brightest yellow of any plant I grow, and they are still good in shade. This has an upright habit, making a clump 80 x 45cm (32 x 18in).

With broader leaves than *C. comans*, *C. morrowii* (Zone 5) has several creamy white variegated varieties such as *C.m.* 'Gilt' (Zone 5) and *C.m.* 'Variegata' (Zone 5). Forming compact evergreen clumps, 45 x 30cm (1½ x 1ft), the white-margined leaves create a very neat effect.

Broader leaves are also produced on *C. siderosticha* 'Variegata' (Zone 6). These are striped and margined in white. This variety forms good low clumps about 15cm (6in) high, spreading slowly and staying attractive all season.

With its fan-shaped leaves and very striking, creamy white variegation,

C. phyllocephala 'Sparkler' (Zone 8) makes a beautiful container plant. Because it is not totally hardy, it requires a little frost protection and will make a clump 60 x 60cm (2 x 2ft).

The same fan-shaped leaf arrangement is also to be found in palm branch sedge (*C. muskingumensis*) (Zone 4). This produces fresh green, highly textured ground cover, 60cm (2ft) high, creeping ever wider, in sun or shade. *C.m.* 'Little Midge' (Zone 4) has the same habit but is smaller, at 30cm (1ft) high.

LUZULA WOOD RUSH

For creating low greenery in difficult shady places, even dry shade, the wood rushes are excellent. Greater wood rush (*L. sylvatica*) (Zone 4) is native to the UK, where it thrives on acid soils mainly in the west and north of the country. It is the most vigorous spreading species of wood rush, quickly producing fresh, dense ground cover 45cm (1½ft) high, through which weeds struggle to get a foothold. Greater wood rush is evergreen in the UK but

deciduous in colder climates. The loose sprays of flowers reach 60cm (2ft) in late spring and are quietly attractive to lovers of chestnut-brown flowers. Its broad, dark green leaves would make a good foil for tall ferns, such as polystichums and dryopteris, which are able to grow above the wood-rush canopy. There is a variegated variety, *L.s.* 'Marginata' (Zone 5), with glossy green leaves, 30cm (1ft) high, edged in creamy yellow ageing to

Luzula sylvatica 'Aurea'

Melica uniflora

white, which is generally a better choice for smaller gardens. Of similar size and equally good is *L.s.* 'Aurea' (Zone 5), which can brighten any shady corner with its golden foliage.

Snowy wood rush (*L. nivea*) (Zone 6) bears white flowers on 60cm (2ft) stems and is gently spreading. The colouring is particularly pure in the closely allied and similar-sized *L. luzuloides* 'Schneehäschen' (Zone 6). This has narrower leaves than greater wood rush and is useful where a large planting is envisaged or as an edging plant in shade.

MELICA MELICK

Wood melick (*M. uniflora*) (Zone 6) is another native of the UK and is one of the most beautiful of woodland grasses. In the wild this grass is often found on steep wood banks especially on limy soils, where its delicate flowering stems are shown to full advantage with their nodding heads of dark, egg-shaped spikelets. This deciduous grass emerges in spring with a thicket of gently arching, fresh green leaves above

which the flowers appear in early summer. It grows to about 30cm (1ft) high and spreads by stolons and by self-seeding.

When planted in shade, wood melick can look fabulous situated where a low morning or evening sun can backlight it. There is a subtle variegated variety, *M.u.* 'Variegata' (Zone 7), which has creamy white, striped leaves and dark spikelets. It is a personal favourite and makes patches 30cm (1ft) square by 25cm (10in) high.

Mountain melick (*M. nutans*) (Zones 6) can grow up to 60cm (2ft) high with a spread of 45cm (1½ft). It has pendulous spikelets held in denser, more upright sprays and a rather upright growth habit. Mountain melick is perfect once again where a low sun can backlight it.

Much taller growing, and to my eye less graceful, is *M. altissima* 'Atropurpurea' (Zone 5), which can reach 1m (3ft) in height by 60cm (2ft) wide. It bears dense upright spikes of purple-brown flowers. This variety is happy to grow in full sun, yet still looks good in shade, where the flower colour is less pronounced but the growth habit more open and elegant.

MILIUM MILLET

The only millet species of interest to the shade gardener is the golden-leaved form of wood millet, *M. effusum* 'Aureum' (Zone 6), or Bowles' golden grass as it is often referred to. This is a beautiful grass, particularly in spring when the new leaves emerge a soft yellow colour. Later in spring, it has open, dainty flower heads that are the same yellow throughout. In heavy shade, the tints will be more green but still provide lovely contrasting colour and texture for other spring-flowering plants. Bowles' golden grass has an upright habit to 60cm (2ft) and a spread of 40cm (16in).

More flowers will be produced in a less shaded position, but the yellow leaves are more likely to get scorched if the site is too hot. This grass can be partially summer dormant when it is under stress; it then dies back to a few, much-reduced leaves. For this reason, it is not a very good plant for container-growing.

Bowles' golden grass seeds true to type and very often the seedlings emerge in very exciting places. I have had this grass turn up among pink dicentras (*see p.30*), blue *Corydalis flexuosa*, yellow *Meconopsis cambrica*, and black-leaved ophiopogon to name but a few. It has looked wonderful wherever it has occurred.

Milium effusum 'Aureum'

Ferns

ADIANTUM MAIDENHAIR FERN
Three main hardy species are invaluable
for the shade gardener. These have fresh
green fronds on dark stems, and
superficially they resemble the tender
maidenhair ferns so popular as houseplants.
All make excellent container plants.

The tallest hardy adiantum is clump-
forming *A. pedatum* (Zone 3), which sends
up a forest of wiry black stems on top of
which the sprays of dainty fronds fan out
to create an umbrella of unparalleled
elegance, some 45 x 45cm (1½ x 1½ft).
Because it is too beautiful to cram in with
equal-sized plants, this fern should be given
a spot among lower-growing plants, where
its shape and form can best be appreciated.

A similar habit and form is shown by
clump-forming *A. aleuticum* (Zone 3). In
A.a. 'Japonicum' (Zone 3) the pink-tinged
young fronds gradually mature to green.
This pink colour can vary in its intensity,
but in the best forms can be a rich copper
shade, which lasts for many weeks. At
30–40cm (12–16in), this variety is a little
smaller than *A. pedatum*. *A. aleuticum*
'Subpumilum' (zone 3) is the smallest form
of this species, growing only 20 x 30cm
(8 x 12in), and in most respects is like a
dwarf version of *A. pedatum*.

The last hardy species is *A. venustum*
(Zone 6), which mildly runs at the root,
thereby creating patches of beautiful
maidenhair fronds 30cm (1ft) high atop

Athyrium niponicum var. *pictum*

Adiantum pedatum

thin black stems. During spring, the new
foliage unfurls yellow-green, tinted brown,
and has few equals for foliage effect at this
time. It slowly makes patches 60cm (2ft) or
more across. Although in milder climates
this fern is nearly evergreen, it is still better
to cut off all of the old foliage at ground
level in late winter, in order to see the new
emerging fronds better.

ATHYRIUM LADY FERN
Lady fern (*A. filix-femina*) (Zone 4) is a
native British fern, growing 1.5 x 0.4m
(5ft x 16in), that has given rise to many
clones and forms over the years. It was
given its common name on account of the
delicacy and lightness of its fronds. This
intricacy reaches high levels in *A.f.-f.*
Plumosum Group (Zone 4) and varieties

such as *A.f.-f.* 'Plumosum Druery' (Zone 4), which produces fresh, incredibly lacy, yellow-green fronds all season in a cool, moist, semi-shaded spot, where lady fern prefers to grow. These two varieties of lady fern grow only 60 x 60cm (2 x 2ft).

The group of athyriums that come from the Orient are very distinctive ferns. The best known, from Japan, is painted lady fern (*A. niponicum* var. *pictum*) (Zone 4), with its fronds coloured in a remarkable combination of grey-green, pewter, and maroon. Named forms of this species are now becoming available, each having different proportions of these basic colours. All these forms, together with the type species, make dense clumps about 30cm (1ft) high and spread slowly. This fern really does like almost complete shade. The best specimens I have ever seen grew under a greenhouse bench, where virtually no sunlight fell on it. In more light, as is so often the case, the colours of painted lady fern are more pronounced, but its overall habit of growth becomes more compact, losing some of the open elegance of shade-grown plants in the process.

A. otophorum (Zone 5) and its more usually seen variety *A.o.* var. *okanum* (Zone 4) are taller ferns with clumps reaching 75 x 60cm (2½ x 2ft) when established. It has the same basic colours of painted lady fern but they are put together rather more genteely, with grey-green fronds and stems and midribs purple-tinted. It also has a more elegant, upright habit. A recent hybrid, *A.* 'Ghost' (Zone 5), has combined this distinctive silver colouring with a vigorous habit and should become a very welcome addition to the shade garden. It is of similar size and habit to *A. otophorum.*

DRYOPTERIS BUCKLER FERN
This large genus of ferns are typically vase-shaped in habit, 60–90cm (2–3ft) high, and are usually strong-growing and easy plants to cultivate. This genus has spawned many varieties, not least from the male fern (*D. filix-mas*) (Zone 2), so-named because of its robustness compared to the equally common, but more delicate-looking, lady

Dryopteris wallichiana

fern (*Athyrium filix-femina*). Male fern is a very accommodating species, thriving in a wide range of soils except boggy ones. It grows quite happily in dense shade. It is best to remove unwanted young male fern plants when tiny, because they grow very rapidly, soon swamping smaller neighbours. They are not that easy to remove when mature.

A better fern for the gardener is golden-scaled male fern (*D. affinis* subsp. *borreri*) (Zone 7), which is semi-evergreen. Its young fronds are a beautiful, golden-green colour and are clothed in golden-brown scales. They mature to a rich green, which remains all season until hard frosts.

Among other species of dryopteris, *D. erythrosora* (Zone 8) has beautiful, orange-rose young fronds, a gently creeping habit, and seems to appreciate a rich cool soil in a sheltered spot. The same conditions are suitable for *D. wallichiana* (Zone 6) from the Orient. This species grows up to 1.5 x 0.75m (5 x 2½ft), and has young fronds, yellow-green on unfurling, covered in black scales. This lends it a very handsome but slightly sinister air. Both of these species are mostly evergreen in sheltered sites. The old fronds are best removed in spring as the new fronds start to expand.

POLYSTICHUM SHIELD FERN
Another large genus of very useful evergreen ferns for shade are shield ferns. The most important species for the gardener is soft shield fern (*P. setiferum*) (Zone 7). At the end of the 19th century, when the fern

craze was at its height, this species alone had given rise to more than 360 varieties, most of which have now disappeared. Those that remain are very tolerant of a wide range of conditions – even dry shade. The mature fronds are dark green. This species looks eye-catching during spring (*below*), once the the previous year's fronds have been cut away. The species and its varieties are typically vase-shaped, up to 1 x 0.75m (3 x 2½ft).

In many varieties, the frond pinnae are divided into smaller segments, and often split again and again (quadripinnate). This gives the fronds a very fine, almost feathery appearance. *P.s.* Divisilobum Group (Zone 7) can be 4-pinnate, and its young foliage is covered in white scales, giving the fern a silvery appearance in spring.

There are still many varieties of soft shield fern worth growing, and one of the very best is *P.s.* 'Pulcherrimum Bevis' (Zone 7). This produces graceful, silky textured fronds with tapering points.

Sword fern (*P. munitum*) (Zone 6), from North America, is one of the very best evergreen ferns. It is vase-shaped with fronds arching at their tips and reaching about 1 x 1m (3 x 3ft). The frond segments are very regular and dark shining green in colour. The whole plant is remarkably elegant for a large fern.

Polystichum setiferum

INDEX